# FANTASY DREAMING

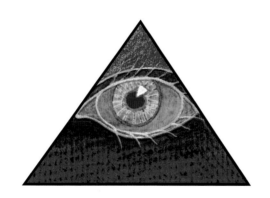

# FANTASY DREAMING

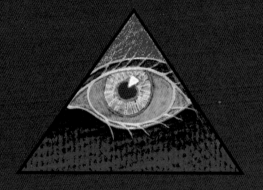

## CRAIG HAMILTON-PARKER

*With illustrations by Steinar Lund and Lynne Milton*

STERLING PUBLISHING CO., INC. • NEW YORK

**Library of Congress Cataloging-in-Publication Data Available**

1  3  5  7  9  10  8  6  4  2

Published by Sterling Publishing Company, Inc.
387 Park Avenue South, New York, N.Y. 10016
© 2002 by Craig Hamilton Parker
Distributed in Canada by Sterling Publishing
c/o Canadian Manda Group, One Atlantic Avenue, Suite 105
Toronto, Ontario, Canada M6K 3E7
Distributed in Australia by Capricorn Link (Australia) Pty. Ltd.
P.O. Box 704, Windsor, NSW 2756 Australia
*Printed in China*

Sterling ISBN 0-8069-5478-7

## Dedication

This book is dedicated to those who have helped make my dreams come true.

Thank you to my wife Jane for her support. Thanks also to Steinar Lund and Lynne Milton for their wonderful illustrations and creative input. Thanks also to Vi Kipling and Caz Cartwright, who have helped build my Internet community, where people can share their dreams and apply counseling techniques suggested in this book.

*"All your dreams can come true...*

*If you have the courage to pursue them."*

**—WALT DISNEY**

# Contents

# Chapter 1

# FANTASY DREAMING

*"Dreams are not meant to put us to sleep, but to awaken us."*

GOEMANS

Imagine you're at home having an argument with someone very close to you. Everything the person says completely undermines you. The person says terribly upsetting things to you: talks about the past, money, sex, children, career, and tells you what an awful person you really are.

The pitch rises. Your heart beats so fast, you can hear it pulsing. Your mouth is dry, your palms sweaty. You are both shouting at each other. Eventually, you reach your limit. Fighting back anger, you storm out of the house and walk or drive to a familiar place where you feel comfortable.

This is an imaginary exercise, but it is a situation you are likely to encounter. If you are like most people, after a fight of this type, you will tend to fantasize about what happened, and the quarrel will continue in your head.

The picture you have in your mind about the other person may have changed, as may have their opinion of you. As you storm down the street you may be thinking about things you said and what you wish you'd said.

You will probably also fantasize about terrible things you would like to do to the person to get revenge. If the fight was extreme, you may think about hurting the person physically or resorting to the law to have your idea of justice carried out. If you are married you may fantasize about divorce and what it would be like if you went your own way.

Eventually you will probably calm down and these extreme fantasies will subside. However, these fantasies will have helped you manage your anger and given you ways to cope without the person who has upset you. If you are inconsolable, you may make one of the fantasies a reality. You may drink too much, take drugs, get involved with the wrong sort of partner, or emotionally punish someone else for your own distress. Often rationality flies out of the window, and afterward you find yourself asking, "Whatever got into me?" or "Why did I do that?"

It is normal for even the best of friends to have an argument. Once the dust dies down, they resolve their dispute and things return to normal. When you again meet the person you had the quarrel with, you will bring with you not only the memory of what was actually said but also the content of your fantasy. You may even in future arguments accuse the person of things that were not actually said but were part of the post-quarrel fantasy you had.

Similarly, the person you quarreled with will also have spent time fantasizing about what happened, and these fantasies will have changed both your moods. Your fantasies may have helped you both resolve the situation or may have made it worse. Whatever the case, you now have to find out where you both stand.

## Fantasy in Everyday Life

The above scenario illustrates how everyone uses fantasy in everyday life. There is nothing weak or foolish about fantasy. Fantasy has a function and is a creative way of thinking. Fantasy can use symbols and imaginary scenarios to solve problems in ways that are different from logic. People who are able to fantasize are often more creative and inventive than people who are primarily rational. Indeed, everything we have today was first conceived in our imagination before it could

become a reality. On an emotional level, fantasy can act as a safety valve, releasing pent-up feelings that cannot normally be expressed in everyday life.

If we can take conscious control of our fantasies, or at the least become more aware of them, we can live more fulfilled and creative lives. We use fantasy all the time but in most instances are unaware that we are doing it. We carry in our minds many pictures of how the world is and how we wish it could be. This is particularly apparent in human relationships. For example, you may know what your partner is really like. You know your partner's strengths and also his or her weaknesses. You know what makes your partner tick, and you know most of your partner's hopes and fears. However, you may also carry a fantasy picture of how you wish your partner would be. You may imagine your partner stronger, more romantic, or more understanding. During intimate moments you may imagine your partner much sexier and more attractive than in reality. Marcel Proust expressed this in an amusing way when he said: "Let us leave pretty women to men without imagination!"

## Projected Fantasy

The truth is, we project onto other people and the world in general our own hidden fantasies. These can be both positive fantasies and negative ones as well. Often, certain individuals can become our bête noire because they come to represent everything we hate about ourselves. We project our fantasies onto them and they are transformed into the scapegoat for our own inadequacies. Similarly, an individual may remind us of someone who wronged us in the past, and we may accuse this unwitting person of the sins of their predecessor.

Fantasy and projected fantasy play a big role when people fall in love. Carl Jung claimed that each of us is psychologically part male and part female. He called these two aspects of the self the Anima (female) and the Animus (male). The Anima and Animus appear in dreams and fantasies as the perfect man or woman. These concepts of the "perfect man" and "perfect woman" are projected onto the opposite sex resulting in the experience of "falling in love." In my own work as a medium and psychic counselor one of the most often asked questions is, "When will I meet 'Mr. Right'?" Clearly, the question itself implies that the woman already has a preconception that there is a "Mr. Right," someone who lives up to her fantasies and expectations. He is the Animus figure that has appeared in her dreams and fantasies. Men have similar preconceptions and speak about "the woman of my dreams."

Fantasies about sex and relationships play a huge role in whom we choose as life partners. Unfortunately these fantasies are usually unrealistic; newlyweds often face a crisis when they begin to distinguish between the person they thought they married and their spouse. Nonetheless, fantasy plays an important role in bonding, and new fantasies gradually replace those that are discarded. All sorts of influences affect the nature of these fantasies, including our early childhood and the image we have of our father, mother, and siblings. Fantasies go on in our minds all the time without our awareness. Sometimes they can be spotted by other people, but often they remain clandestine.

Within this book, you will read about sexual fantasies and about how these influence relationships. You will also read about how fantasy influences other aspects of our life, such as work, ambition, creativity, escapism, anxiety, and spirituality. I will also demonstrate how advertising and marketing influence and take advantage of your fantasies to sell you products. (Before becoming a full-time writer and Spiritualist medium, I was the managing director of an advertising agency.)

Fantasy is a powerful psychological force that reveals a great deal about your desires and aspirations. Much of the time you are unaware of the existence of these fantasies, so you are susceptible to persuasion. You could also become the victim of your own delusions or the influence-wielding tactics of other people. Mindfulness of our fantasies and their meaning can make us more self-aware and more resistant to manipulation.

## DAYDREAMS

*"All men dream: but not equally.*
*Those who dream by night in the dusty*
*recesses of their mind wake up in the day*
*to find that it was vanity; but the*
*dreamers of the day are dangerous men,*
*for they may act their dream with*
*open eyes, to make it possible."*

T. E. LAWRENCE,
LAWRENCE OF ARABIA

Fantasy is a way of thinking. I would call it semi-unconscious thinking, for much of the time we only become aware that we are having a fantasy once it has already started.

Sometimes we call it daydreaming. It is a state of mind somewhere between sleeping and waking.

Daydreams are close to conscious thought, and we can usually choose whether to have them or not. They can be a very creative tool and may help to calm a troubled mind or bring to awareness creative ideas and solutions to problems. As children at school we were told not to daydream. This admonition may have served only to deny us an important and useful function of the brain. Charles Dickens wrote most of his best work after a period of light reverie. Mozart, Napoleon, and Edison were all known to catnap to solve problems and restore their drive. They all slept less than five hours a night.

Fantasy can be effective when you allow yourself to catnap for five minutes during the day. Although you do not usually fall into a deep sleep you do, however, tap the hidden working of the unconscious and can pull interesting ideas into the light of consciousness. Daydreaming during a catnap can also be deeply relaxing and restorative as it gives the mind a chance to use dream functions to help you to stop emotionally overheating.

Try this simple exercise to help you to use daydream fantasy.

### EXERCISE

## DAYDREAMING

**Step 1:** Put your feet up or sit in a chair and relax. It's best not to lie down or you may fall asleep. A good time to do this exercise is during a coffee break or at a time when your mind is very active. Allow your breathing to slow down and feel all the tension of the day fall away. You feel deeply relaxed. Notice how as the breathing slows down your mind becomes quieter. Notice how good you feel.

**Step 2:** Your subconscious mind is still working to find solutions to the problems of the day. These may be creative problems, intellectual ones, or emotional difficulties you need to resolve. If you have a particular worry on your mind, let it come to the surface. Mentally examine the problem for a while as if it is something separate from yourself. Don't get tangled up with it or worry about it; simply look at it with detached attention. You are now going to let your daydreaming mind give you a solution to the problems you have encountered.

**Step 3:** Now let go of the problem, knowing the unconscious mind will eventually sort it out and may be able to give you solutions to your difficulties very soon. You may want to see the problem symbolically falling away from you. For example, you may imagine a heavy, textured rock falling away from you like an asteroid disappearing into outer space. You can hear it rushing away.

**Step 4:** Give yourself permission to think about anything you like. This is your time. You may want to think about nothing in particular and just enjoy the relaxed state you are inducing. Watching the breath can help increase your relaxation. With every exhalation, let your body and mind relax more deeply.

**Step 5:** When you are ready, become aware of the pictures and thoughts that naturally arise in your mind's eye. If none come to you, don't worry: you are benefiting from this period of relaxation anyway. If you do see an image, look closely at it. It may be a static image or it may be animated in some way. Increase you awareness of what you are seeing by looking for colors, textures, and sounds associated with the image. Let all your senses get involved.

**Step 6**: You will find that one image will encourage another to arise. And another and another. Gradually, a whole stream of pictures may be seen in the mind's eye until you enter a dreamlike state of awareness. Yet you are not asleep, as you have conscious control over what is happening. Don't worry about what the pictures mean. Just enjoy watching them. It is incredible how these pictures that arise spontaneously from this simple mental exercise can be full of wonderful detail and complexity.

**Step 7**: When you feel that the subconscious has done its work, open your eyes and immediately write down the most important images you saw. If you lapsed into a sequence of events, write them down as if you were writing down a dream you just had. Add as much detail as you can. Don't worry about sequence, spelling, or grammar.

**Step 8**: Now examine the material you have gathered. Among the fantasy material may be some obvious ideas that relate to your problems. You may be able to spot these immediately as ways to deal with your difficulty. However many of the fantasies and images are symbols. They represent solutions to your problems and give you allegorical answers that may need a little interpretation. You can look these up in this book in the sections that follow or in the index to learn some of the meanings of these images. Remember, however, that symbols can have many layers of meaning, so use this book as a guide, but most of all trust what your own instincts tell you.

What you have just done is to use daydreaming to access the unconscious mind. During normal waking life we only use about 10 percent of our brain. By calling on the powers of the unconscious mind you open up all sorts of new possibilities. You can use this technique to help you solve your problems—and you can even become a genius!

## UNCONSCIOUS FANTASY

*"The faculty of imagination is both the rudder and the bridle of the senses."*

LEONARDO DA VINCI

The last exercise combined conscious and unconscious fantasy dreams. However we all also have fantasies working in the background of our mind—and of which we are almost completely unaware.

These hidden fantasies have an influence on us. Without realizing it, we are living a fantasy. Some people become so wrapped up in their fantasy experience, it becomes integral to their life. For example as I write this, my immediate neighborhood feels a sense of celebration, because a woman who made trouble for everyone has moved away. Her life was so shallow that she ruled the neighborhood tyrannically. Harboring fantasies of power and conquest, she expressed them as complaints about everybody and everything. Perhaps you know people like this: traffic cops who behave like stormtroopers, executives who expect to be judged by the size of their car, and homemakers who decorate a cottage as if it were the Palace of Versailles.

Everywhere you look, people live out their fantasies in ordinary life. In most instances, they are completely unaware of what they are doing. Have you ever noticed that during an argument with someone they accuse you of the very faults that are their own? Or maybe you are accused of breaking promises you never actually made? The fantasies we have about ourselves and the people around us are for the most part unconscious. We sometimes laugh when we see a person locked into one of these illusions but to some extent we are all motivated by unconscious conceptions of whom we would like to be.

It is interesting to watch the people around you and ask yourself what fantasy motivates this person or that. Often groups of people get sucked into a collective fantasy. For example consider the fantasies that accompanied the rise of Hitler. Nazi films and propaganda were filled with references to myths and stories that appealed to a very deep strata of the unconscious mind. The German became the heroic Teutonic knight, and the Jews and Gypsies became the scapegoats for everything that was wrong with the world. Today we can still see similar heroic fantasies at work in totalitarian and repressive governments. Often these fantasies center around the "beloved leader" who becomes the heroic figure representing everything we wish to be ourselves.

You may recognize collective fantasy in your immediate environment or in the news. For example, the spate of recent conspiracy theories may reveal a deep-seated insecurity in Western consciousness. This collective fantasy shows that people feel their lives are out of control. They have a lack of trust in the world and a fear of society.

We will consider many more unconscious fantasies throughout this book. From a personal standpoint, becoming aware of your fantasies and their meanings will enable you to become more conscious of what hopes and fears motivate you. Throughout the sections of this book I suggest alternative fantasies that you may deliberately induce to give yourself a more positive mental attitude. These are like a living affirmation to enable you to influence the unconscious in a positive way. The objective of this is to help you use fantasy to achieve greater psychological stability and increase your confidence.

The exercise that follows will help you to become more aware of some of your unconscious fantasies.

EXERCISE

### UNCONSCIOUS FANTASY

From time to time you may find yourself humming a tune, or you may find you have a song on your mind. Often these melodies arise because you recently heard them. If you think about it, you may be able to remember when. But sometimes songs pop into your head for no apparent reason. With a little thought you can discover the fantasy that lies behind it.

**Step 1:** Think about the last time you heard a song or tune playing in your head. In particular, think about the last occasion a song you hadn't actually heard popped into your head. Write it down on a piece of paper.

**Step 2:** Now write down how you were feeling at the time. Did you start singing it after a particular event? Did something someone said trigger the tune? If you woke up with the music on your mind, can you remember the dream you were having? Make a note of all the things that may have prompted the song. Write them down.

**Step 3:** Now write down the title of the song, the name of the singer/s and also any lines from the song that particularly played on your mind or feel significant to you. Maybe a particular verse or chorus line feels important.

**Step 4:** In a great many cases you will find that the song is associated with something that has been on your mind. It may not be the whole song but the title or the first line may be a reflection of your hidden thoughts. Even the name of the singer may be a message about the way you are feeling. For example, a song by Frank Sinatra may mean that you should be more "frank" with yourself about your "sins" (Sin-atra). The unconscious disguises messages in complicated and ingenious ways.

**Step 5:** Consider the words of the song and the title to see what things they reveal about you. Many of the lyrics may represent things you dare not think about consciously. Deeply hidden fantasies may be disguised through seemingly innocuous music. Perhaps the words say something about how you feel about yourself or your attitude toward others. Do the words hint at your resentments, hopes, fears, and anxieties? Sometimes they may express how you feel about yourself and your place in the world. Maybe the words provide clues to new ways of behaving or attitudes to adopt. If you are working on a problem, creative ideas may be masked in the words of the song.

Fantasies go on in our heads without our being completely aware of them or how they come about. These hidden fantasies are functioning below normal awareness. We can see them at work when we look at cumulus clouds floating through a clear blue sky. It is likely that you will see shapes of faces and fantastic landscapes in the random white shapes of the puffy clouds. One person may see one thing and another may see something completely different. What you see is really a reflection of your own hidden thinking that you are now expressing as visual fantasies projected onto the random shapes of the clouds. The pictures are symbols arising from the unconscious and reveal your hidden emotions, feelings, and thoughts.

As I stated earlier, hidden fantasies often express themselves in our behavior and expectations. We also use fantasy to make sense of other people's behavior and feelings. For example a statement such as "You are just like your mother!" may reveal all sorts of hidden anxieties and preconceptions. On one level the accuser is trying to make sense of the other person's behavior. It may also reveal a child-like resentment toward the other person's mother. The fantasy of the mother involves presumed motivations and often predictions for future expectations. We use unconscious fantasy to explain all sorts of things that we cannot make sense of.

## CONSCIOUS FANTASY

*"The man who has no imagination has no wings."*

MUHAMMAD ALI

Of course one of the functions of fantasy is to enable us to escape from the tedium of our ordinary lives. Fantasy releases us from the banal world of work and responsibility and also compensates for our own weaknesses and inadequacies. For example, when we visit the cinema, read a novel, or even watch some advertisements, we are temporarily transported to another world where we are the invincible hero, the perfect lover, the powerful ruler, or have the perfect family. Fantasy lifts us out of ourselves. For a short while, the worries of real life disappear.

Naturally the content of the fantasies we subject ourselves to can have a powerful influence on our own unconscious fantasies. Walt Disney's work has such a tremendous appeal because many of his finest movies are based upon very old myths and stories that express the perennial hopes and fears of all humans. However, we do not feel comfortable about allowing children to watch pornography or explicit violence because it can cause psychological harm. Yet many adults enjoy extreme fantasies of sex and violence. Also fantasy can give us unrealistic expectations. A man may expect all women to look like magazine models, and a woman may expect a man to be continuously romantic and loving.

Are we encouraging the right sort of fantasies to help ourselves become better people? Most people would agree that extreme and unrestricted fantasy—the fantasies of a pedophile, for example—are not good for a person's well-being. Many fantasies we see in movies can also have a corrupting influence on some personalities. Similarly we are often spoon-fed fantasies through advertising, whose sole purpose is to sell things to us.

Fantasy clearly is a powerful force that can be used to good purpose or as a means of manipulation and corruption. Fantasies that arise spontaneously say a great deal about the psychological influences and motivations that are functioning in the background of your consciousness. However, fantasy can also be used in an active way to deliberately influence the way you feel about yourself and your place in the world. They can be a way of influencing the biological computer called the mind. By using fantasy in a positive way, you can develop a more positive mental attitude and gain greater self-confidence and intellectual prowess. Fantasy can help achieve just about anything. Whether you are practicing an imaginary golf swing in your head, generating ideas, or dealing with emotional worry, fantasy can help you to achieve your objectives.

To demonstrate the power of fantasy and visualization, we will now try a simple experiment in fantasy to demonstrate how it can even influence involuntary bodily processes.

FANTASY PHYSIQUE

## CONSCIOUS FANTASY

**Step 1:** Imagine that you are holding a fresh yellow lemon. You can feel its waxy texture in your hand. Close your eyes and concentrate on this feeling for a while.

**Step 2:** See yourself bringing the lemon up to your nose so that you can smell its crisp zest.

**Step 3:** Now imagine opening your mouth wide and taking a bite of this pungent lemon. Taste how sharp the acid is as your teeth break through the skin of the lemon. As the cold juice touches your mouth, you wince at its tart taste.

**Step 4:** Close your eyes and fully imagine this experience.

**Step 5:** You will find that your mouth is full of saliva.

Using the power of fantasy, you have influenced an involuntary bodily process. If someone had suggested that you fill your mouth with saliva you would not have known how to do it. But using the power of the imagination it is possible to influence the body in remarkable ways.

Imaginative fantasy can be used in similar ways to help the body heal itself. Successful results have been achieved with cancer patients who use the power of conscious fantasy to bring themselves back to good health.

They may, for example, imagine healing light flooding their body, or an army of white blood cells attacking and defeating an army of black, cancerous cells.

So often people get into bad habits and use negative fantasy to trip themselves up. You may for instance pull yourself into a pit of difficulties because of the language you use. People talk themselves ill with phrases such as: "I always catch other people's colds" or "It'll be the death of me...." Such phrases set up negative unconscious thought habits that undermine your positive outlook.

Conscious fantasy can be used to break bad habits and improve your emotional, mental, and spiritual well-being. And positive fantasies will help you access positive energy levels. For instance, if something needs to be done, don't concentrate on the problem, concentrate on the solution. Fantasize about it being resolved and see how easy it is to deal with your difficulties. This attitude stimulates the spiritual energy you need, and the fantasy gives you an unconscious feeling of self-confidence and the desire to proceed. In most instances, worry results from a feeling of loss of control. Conscious fantasy can help break this pattern of behavior.

The more you practice helpful thought patterns and access positive energy levels, the easier it becomes, because the unconscious mind understands repetition and establishes this new behavior programming. Positive fantasies are a powerful spiritual tool. A good film will make you laugh, cry, feel fear, and excite you in different ways. In the same way, the imagery, sounds, and feelings that are running inside you have a powerful influence on your state of mind. So pick the right movies to screen in your inner cinema: in other words, think with positive, confidence-building images, sounds, and feelings that inspire you toward happiness and success.

## PSYCHOLOGY AND FANTASY

*"Dreams are true while they last, and do we not live in dreams?"*

ALFRED LORD TENNYSON

The various schools of psychology have different theories about the nature and role of fantasy. Some point out that sexual desire and aggressive impulses can be satiated by conscious fantasy. These fantasies can be as pleasurable, explicit, or frightening as we want them to be. Many psychologists say that fantasies are a safety net, holding unpleasant aspects of the self in check.

Psychoanalysts categorize fantasies into various types. These include daydreaming and imagining, which also corresponds to neurotic daydreaming. They also speak of unconscious "phantasy" (with a "ph"), which is an imaginative activity that underlies all thought and feeling. (I have already spoken about this concept; for simplicity, I prefer to call it "unconscious fantasy.") All psychodynamic schools agree that conscious mental activity is accompanied, supported, and enriched by unconscious phantasy. In particular, Sigmund Freud observed that these might be oral, anal, libidinal, infantile, or hysterical. Developing this idea, psychoanalyst Melanie Klein pioneered analysis of phantasies that originate during early childhood and are brought forward into adult life.

Analytical psychologist Carl Jung also said that unconscious phantasy developed in childhood and could sometimes be a cause of neurosis or could hinder the growth of the personality. Fantasy arises spontaneously as a safety valve to help the infant to deal with real conflicts in the family, conflicts that may be too difficult or too painful to deal with directly. Jung observed that childhood fantasies include many mythical themes that may be inherent in everyone.

Gestalt psychology, developed by Franz Perls, sees fantasy as a middle zone of consciousness. In fantasy we are trying to make real our self-image rather than our true self, and this distorts and prohibits real psychological growth. These fantasies are characterized by internal debate and are a substitute for dealing with the problems of the real situation. Fantasies negate the future by imagining catastrophic or over-optimistic scenarios. This mental activity can often induce anxiety.

## FANTASY DREAMS

*"The debt we owe to the play of imagination is incalculable."*

CARL JUNG

In dreams, fantasy is unrestricted. Except in lucid dreams, no conscious control exists. Moral judgment is suspended in dreaming, and fantasies can often become shocking or extreme. Dreams reveal your most secret fantasies. They are allegories, symbols, and metaphors that express the way you feel, and they can help you solve emotional difficulties. Fantasies experienced in dreams say a great deal about you and can help you tackle problems you might normally push to the back of your mind. If you understand the inner conditions these fantasy dreams are describing, you can gain important insight into yourself. Dreams highlight problems but also can give solutions to problems. They can show you psychological qualities that inhibit your progress and thereby help you discover new approaches to old problems. Dreams help you change.

Dreams also use fantasy to help solve practical problems. Perplexing intellectual conundrums can be solved in dreams, and many great scientific inventions and creative ideas have come about as the result of dreams. For example, Jules Verne, Charlotte Brontë, Graham Greene, and Robert Louis Stevenson are among the thousands of authors whose work has been inspired by dreams. Countless artists use dreams in their work. The Surrealist movement, which included artists such as Salvador Dali, Max Ernst, and René Magritte, was based on their work on dream images. Great music has sometimes been heard in dreams, and dreams have inspired philosophers, mathematicians, generals, and political leaders. Even the rational worlds of science and engineering owe a great deal to dream fantasies. Physicist Niels Bohr was trying to understand the nature of the atom. One night he dreamed of a sun composed of burning gases with planets orbiting it attached by fine threads. When he awoke he realized that

this was the solution to his puzzle. It explained the structure of the atom and heralded the birth of atomic physics.

Dreams can help psychologically, but they are also a practical, intellectual tool. This ability of the mind to fantasize, and particularly to fantasize in the unrestricted state of dreaming, may be one of the greatest intellectual assets we have.

Dreams, fantasy, and imagination are all part of this wonderful creative ability of the mind to solve problems in a direct way. Often that ability can give insight and understanding when reason and logic founder.

## Working with Your Dreams and Fantasies

To work with dreams it is necessary to start remembering them. I have written extensively about this in *Remembering Your Dreams* and also about how to interpret dreams in *The Hidden Meaning of Dreams.* In my other books I have suggested many ways to recall dreams. By far the best and simplest is to keep a journal.

In this instance I would suggest that you not only keep note of your dreams but also log your fantasies. Like dreams, fantasies contain symbolism and hidden meanings that say a great deal about what is going on below your conscious awareness. Once you know the reasons for your fantasies, you can develop new ones to use as animated affirmations to help you build a positive attitude.

But first here are a few very simple tips to help you improve your ability to remember your dreams:

## DREAM RECALL TIPS

**Keep a fantasy dream journal.** If you write down your dreams immediately upon awakening, you are much more likely to remember your dreams. You need to do this immediately upon awakening, so have a notebook and a pen by the side of your bed. If you wait even just five minutes, you will find that most of your dream has faded from consciousness.

**Don't worry about grammar and spelling when you write.** Also don't bother trying to get the sequences in order. Just get everything you can onto the page. If you do this on a regular basis you will have many dreams you can check in the pages that follow. Your ability to recall dreams will greatly improve over time. If you cannot remember having a dream, write down your thoughts or even a fantasy about what you would have liked to have dreamed. By doing this you get into the habit of trying to recall your dreams. The fantasy you write down may also reveal something about yourself when you look up its meaning in the following chapters.

**Include your fantasies.** If you keep a comparatively small notebook you could carry it with you and occasionally also note your fantasies. Although many of these will be created consciously you may find material that pops into your head seemingly from nowhere. This shows that the unconscious mind is using your conscious fantasy to make you aware of the hidden feelings and thoughts in your mind. Often this material will be in symbols that can be interpreted in the same way you would interpret a dream.

**Consider other people's fantasies.** It is interesting to make a note of the fantasies you notice other people have and how these fantasies influence the way some people interact with others. In particular you may notice that certain fantasies come into play when people communicate with you. For example, who does the boss think she is? What power symbols does she keep in her office? What do her clothes and car say about the way she feels about herself? It is particularly interesting to watch people when they are dancing. In this uninhibited situation they express many of the fantasies about who they would like to be. In these displays, people often express their unconscious fantasies. People live out their self-image in everyday life. Note examples in your journal.

**Note the words.** As soon as you wake from a dream write down any words you specifically heard in the dream. This information is likely to fade from your mind first.

**Lie still.** It has been found that most people change position immediately upon awakening. It is best to remain in the same position when you awaken and try to relive the dream you were having. If you can't recall the dream, change position. This will stimulate a different brain wave pattern and may spontaneously generate dream images.

**Doodle.** Dreams often come to mind when you doodle. Doodles also contain interesting fantasies about the way you feel. For example, if, as you speak to someone on the telephone, you find yourself drawing crosses, it may suggest that you believe the other person is wrong in what he says.

**Talk to your dreams.** Personify your dream and imagine it as a person who does not want to talk to you. Ask the dream person if he will help you to remember your dream. Now relax and let the dream come to you. Imagine that the dream person is telling you about your dream. What starts as a fantasy will eventually reveal the dream you were having.

**Notice your mood.** If you don't remember the events or images from the dream, pay attention to your mood. Indulge in the mood for a while. Does this mood remind you of anything from your dream?

**Start now.** If you apply the above tips and keep a notebook or journal of your dreams and fantasies, you will soon have a great deal of interesting material to work with. If you can remember dreams and fantasies from long ago, note these in your book, too. They will give you an interesting insight into your hopes and fears from that period of your life. Have you got over the problems or do they still lurk in the background of your consciousness? Or

perhaps there are dreams and fantasies that you have forgotten about but could enrich your life now. For example perhaps you once had fantasies about being a pop star, artist, or writer. Although you may no longer have the opportunity to fulfill these desires, you may find many other ways to express your neglected creative or intellectual urges.

## UNDERSTANDING DREAMS AND FANTASIES

*"Imagination is more important than knowledge."*

ALBERT EINSTEIN

There are many theories about the role of dreams and fantasies, but most agree that dreams and fantasies are the link between the conscious mind and the unconscious. Without them we would probably overheat emotionally and never be able to cope with the complexities of life. Dreams give the brain the opportunity to explore its potential in ways that would never be possible in day-to-day life. Dreams and fantasies show us new ways of doing things and help us scale the evolutionary ladder.

It is generally agreed that dreams and fantasies are essential for health. As an emotional safety valve, dreams are as important to our well-being as eating and drinking; without them, frustration and anxiety would overwhelm us. Similarly conscious fantasy, which is a superficial form of dreaming, may help relieve the stress caused by the banality of everyday life.

Dreams and fantasies also help you assimilate knowledge and learn. A fantasy may reveal solutions to a problem more quickly than rational thought. As has been shown, dreams have been responsible for many creative ideas and inventions. In particular, dreams can show solutions to personal dilemmas and prepare you for the future. They expose your deepest fears and signpost ways to resolve these fears.

Dreams and fantasies express emotions, feelings, and abstract ideas in the language of symbols. Symbols are a very flexible way of thinking and mean many things to different people. For example, to one person, an apple may represent good health, to another it may be the brand name of their computer; another may be reminded of wholeness; another may see it as a symbol of Eve's temptation or as the forbidden knowledge of sexuality. Just about anything can be symbolic, and the meaning may have many individual slants.

Every dream and fantasy you have is unique to you, but many themes occur that other people have as well. For example, a child's *Star Wars* fantasy of being a Jedi knight or being a comic book superhero is in essence the same as the fantasies children had in ancient times. Ancient Greek children may have imagined themselves as Perseus slaying the snake-headed Gorgon; a Viking child would have played at being Beowulf; and a Mesopotamian child probably fantasized about being Gilgamesh. If you read these ancient tales, you will see many similarities to the most popular films and stories of today. Although we may think our fantasies and dreams are unique, at a primal level they correspond with fantasies people have had for millennia.

Myths and legends have such similar characters and themes, they would appear to be penned by the same author. These traditions arise because on a deep psychological level people share similar memories, the foundations of which go back far into ancient history to the times when humanity was just beginning to attain consciousness. The archaic memories cross all cultural boundaries and show how humanity is connected by an inherent spirituality. Myths and legends are just like dreams and fantasy in that they express the human condition by weaving stories through an association of symbols. And they continue to be fascinating today. Many sensible people fantasize about ancient Egypt and in some cases believe that they are incarnations of Egyptian priests, priestesses, or pharaohs. Who is to say it is a fantasy? Perhaps many fantasies about ancient times and other cultures are real memories that express themselves in fantasy.

By studying your dreams and fantasies, you can see many symbolic stories that express the motivating forces in your life. Work with these unconscious forces to improve your life.

Although many people have the same dreams and fantasies, the symbolism of the dream fantasy will be unique and personal. As you begin to see what is working below the surface of your consciousness, you will be

ARCHETYPAL MEMORIES FROM ANCIENT EGYPT

able to understand why you are having particular dream fantasies.

### SOMETHING TO REMEMBER

You may think you never dream or that you dream only occasionally, but tests have shown that everybody dreams every night. People tend to forget dreams upon awakening. Here are some simple ways to help you remember you dreams:

**Interrupt a dream.** On average, people dream every 90 minutes. The longest dreams, lasting 30 to 40 minutes, occur in the morning. Setting your alarm slightly earlier than usual may help awaken you just as a dream ends and while it's still clear in your mind.

**Write it down.** Most dreams are forgotten within 10 minutes, so start writing down your dream as soon as you wake up. Give the dream a title, then list everything you can remember, no matter how unimportant it may seem. Note the day and date as well; it may be useful later, particularly if your dream tells the future.

**Talk about it.** It's amazing how many extra details surface if you tell someone your dream. The other person may also be able to help with interpretation. A chance remark can "crack the code."

**Flashbacks.** Fragments of a dream may recur during the day; make note of them if they do.

**Fantasy.** Fantasies during the day may remind you of your dream from the previous night. Fantasies are like dreams in that they can show what is going on in your unconscious. Write down your fantasies, talk about them with your friends, and when a fantasy recurs, note what triggers it. What causes you to have the fantasy, and what does your fantasy say about your emotional response?

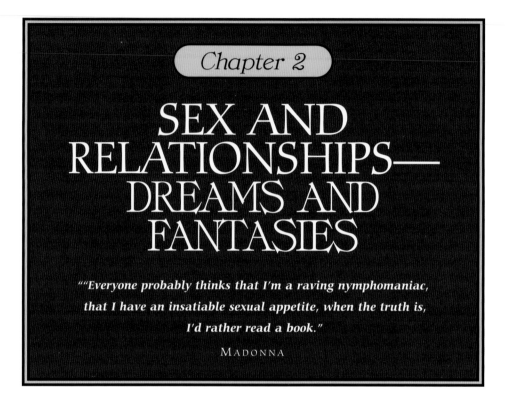

# Chapter 2

# SEX AND RELATIONSHIPS— DREAMS AND FANTASIES

*""Everyone probably thinks that I'm a raving nymphomaniac, that I have an insatiable sexual appetite, when the truth is, I'd rather read a book."*

MADONNA

Sigmund Freud revolutionized the way we think about ourselves and our attitudes toward sex. His psychoanalytic terms such as id, ego, libido, neurosis, transference, fixation, and Oedipus complex have become part of our everyday language. In particular, he believed that "all dreams represent the fulfillment of wishes" and that their function provides systematic evidence for the unconscious. According to Freud, wish fulfillment in dreams and fantasies is usually (but not always) sexual in

nature. Usually the wish within the dream is hidden, disguised, or distorted. Disguised sexual themes will often occur in dreams and fantasies and we will consider some of these in this section.

Sigmund Freud is generally recognized as one of the most influential and authoritative thinkers of the twentieth century. He was working at a time when sexual matters were never talked about openly. Some of his most important theories were conceived at a time when Queen Victoria sat on the

English throne, and Chester A. Arthur was the president of the United States. During these conservative times, Freud was to propose psychological theories utterly shocking to society in general.

One of his most important theoretical breakthroughs came soon after 1882, while he lived in Vienna. At the time he worked closely with the respected physician, Josef Breuer, and investigated an interesting case of hysteria. The woman in question (known as Anna O) had a strict upbringing and was suffering from acute anxieties that affected her behavior and, as Freud was to discover, resulted in a severe nervous cough, a squint, visual disturbances, and most importantly, paralysis of the right arm. Breuer and Freud found that by getting Anna O to talk about her condition and investigating the memories associated with such things as her fear of water, they were able to cure not only her anxiety but the physical disabilities as well. Anna O's real name was Bertha Pappenheim (1859-1936). She recovered and became a leading social worker and feminist.

Freud surmised that many of the symptoms were a result of traumatic (trauma is the Greek for "wound") experiences from Anna's past and that these symptoms disappeared when traced back to their first occasion. Symptoms were removed by recalling forgotten unpleasant events, but they emerged with the greatest force when they were being talked away. The result of these investigations was a book by Freud and Breuer, *Studies in Hysteria* (1895). The "talking cure" was the first step toward the therapeutic treatments we use today.

What shocked society at the time was Freud's conclusion that the ideas people resisted the most were sexual in nature. The Anna O case, he argued, had a sexual basis. He argued that repressed memories nearly always revealed seduction or sexual molestation by a parent or adult. Also, traumatic childhood events operated in a delayed way. Repressed memories could become pathogenic ideas and cause hysterical symptoms after puberty. Armed with this knowledge, Freud was able to begin treating neuroses and help his patients to resolve their sexual problems.

Although much of Freud's work was with people who had psychological problems, he was in fact interested in a general theory of the mind. Many of Freud's ideas have today been superseded by new theories, but there is still a lot to learn from his discoveries. In particular, Freud understood that people repress unpleasant ideas and that in many cases these ideas are sexual in origin. Society today is more open-minded than in Freud's time; nonetheless sexual themes continue to appear in fantasies and dreams in a disguised/symbolic form as well as openly.

Freud's innovative treatments have proven to be extraordinarily durable. His most important claim, however, that with psychoanalysis he had invented a new science of the mind, remains the subject of much critical debate and controversy.

The other great early pioneer of the unconscious mind was Swiss psychologist Carl Jung, initially a pupil of Freud's. Freud hoped Jung would continue his work and carry the baton of psychoanalysis after Freud's death. However, Jung began to have serious doubts. In particular, Jung proposed that sexual trauma was not the only cause of neurosis. He pointed out that there was scarcely a human being who has not had some sexual shocks in early youth and yet comparatively few developed neuroses in later life. He was critical of Freud's insistence that the existence of infantile sexual fantasies was the root cause of most psychological problems and fixations. Jung believed that neurosis was only partly due to early infantile predisposition and that it also had causes in the present as well.

To the dismay of the dogmatic Freud, Jung proposed that his psychoanalytic theory be freed from the purely sexual standpoint. In place of it he argued for a theory based on an energetic viewpoint.

Freud had defined the libido as the sexual desires that motivate the human condition. "Libido" in common usage now means sexual impulses. However, Jung preferred to use it in its original sense as "desire," including all types of desire, not just sexual. Libido is the life force, but this only slowly develops into a sexual impulse. In short, Jung claimed that the causes of neurosis lay not in the past but in the present.

Jung began to use the word "libido" as a synonym for psychic energy in general, whereas Freud used it to signify only sexual energy. Similarly, Jung argued that not all fantasies should be interpreted literally. For example, Freud believed that neurosis was connected with the persistence of incestuous desires connected with the Oedipus complex (a person's desire to seduce his mother). Jung, however, argued that these fantasies might be spiritual symbols. Jung said that incest signified a personal complication only in the rarest cases. Usually incest has a highly religious aspect, for which reason the incest theme plays a decisive part in almost all cosmologies and in numerous myths. But Freud clung to the literal interpretation of it and could not grasp the spiritual significance of incest as a "symbol."

Jung's notion of psychic energy was also more extensive than Freud's. Libido is an energy that moves between instinct and what Jung called *archetype:* between body and spirit. According to Jung, sex in a dream may represent the basic instinct of sexual desire itself or conversely the ultimate image of connectedness. The sexual act symbolizes the union of opposites. Jung also wrote of "grand dreams," meaning dreams filled with a sense of the numinous and the spiritual. Sexual dreams may be the "grand dreams" of the body, which connect the spiritual aspect of a person with their earthly nature.

Clearly psychological interpretation of fantasy and dreams was now following divergent pathways. Today there is still great controversy about Freud and the new theories that have their roots in psychoanalysis.

# SEXUAL FANTASIES

*"Sex appeal is fifty percent what you've got and fifty percent what people think you've got."*

SOPHIA LOREN

In Greece they have a saying: "When the candle is taken away, every woman is alike" and similarly in Australia they say, "All women look the same with a sack over their heads." And of course you can say exactly the same about men!! Few people actually look like the well-toned movie stars and advertising models we are expected to aspire to be like. The fact is, the attractiveness of your partner is not determined entirely by physical appearance but by your imagination. Add the ingredient of fantasy and your love life is bound to improve.

Similarly from the body's point of view an orgasm is just an orgasm. It's a physical function just like any other. But good sex is pure fantasy. Sex happens inside the mind. It is what makes lovemaking exciting and fun. There are common fantasies that many confess to enjoying, and there are also wilder ones that may not suit everyone. In fantasy, you may try things you wouldn't contemplate doing in real life. Some common fantasies include being in a threesome, being watched, or having sex in a public place. Some people fantasize about being tied up, beating or being beaten, being taken by force, or having sex with a stranger. Many enjoy the thought of having sex with a favorite movie or pop star or having sex in a dangerous situation.

It is normal to have sexual fantasies. These are different for each individual. What one person may enjoy another may find unpleasant or upsetting. Many psychologists, particularly those from the Freudian tradition, believe that the origins of sexual fantasies can be traced to early childhood. You may find it helpful to act on your sexual fantasies, but do it by choice—because you want to, not because you are out of control and you feel compelled to or because your partner has radically different fantasies from your own.

# SEXUAL FANTASY DREAMS

*"Talking from morning to night about sex has helped my skiing, because I talk about movement, about looking good, about taking risks."*

RUTH WESTHEIMER

According to Freud, all dream activity relates in some way to sex. Most people would consider this an extreme point of view, but it is true that sexual imagery is a vital part of dream content. Dreams have a lot to teach you about your sexual nature, your fears, and your anxieties.

Dreams are a rich source of fantasy and can be a way to deal with unfulfilled desires from waking life. Also, as dreams are messages from the unconscious mind, they can reveal our deep feelings and our true motivations. In particular, they can bring to light many repressed sexual desires, our guilty feelings or our unexpressed fears about sex.

If a person has a high degree of repression, the person's fears and anxieties may be expressed through their dreams. Similarly, the person's desire for greater fulfillment may be expressed in erotic dreams. If the sexual repression is severe, the dreams may be filled with sexual situations that the person would find shocking, embarrassing, or confusing. In such cases, there is often a big difference between the person's waking sexuality and the sexuality displayed in dreams. The person's day-to-day life may be emotionally sterile and sensually barren, but the dream life is full of eroticism and steamy sexual encounters. By paying attention to your dreams you can learn about your needs and desires and perhaps discover ways to make your life more sensual if necessary.

Your sexual dreams may also reveal things about the way you feel about your relationships and your shared sexual behavior. As was explained in the section about Freud, dreams can sometimes disguise sexual subjects and wrap the naked truth in all manner of symbolism. Explicit sexual images may appear in dreams. For example, should you dream of having sex with a member of your family or someone completely inappropriate, it does not necessarily mean that you have a mixed-up sexuality. Psychologists point out that this type of dream can be a symbolic message about your relationship with these people. You may worry that you have these illicit feelings, but dreams of this nature are comparatively common. There's no need to panic. Don't read too much into them.

Erotic dreams usually occur at times when you need a certain amount of release from tension. They are a safety valve that lets out your pent-up frustrations and sexual inhibitions. They may compensate for your unfulfilled sex. People who have balanced and happy sex lives in their waking life do not, as a general rule, dream about sex. As far as we know, the primary functions of dreams are to maintain sleep and prevent the brain from emotionally overheating. Dreams therefore are often concerned with resolving problems and restoring emotional equilibrium. If sexual issues are important to you or have been pushed out of your waking consciousness, your dreams will try to deal with these unresolved issues. Even nightmares can be therapeutic, as they draw to your attention many of the hidden fears that may be preventing you from moving forward. Pay attention to your dreams and nightmares; they may hold the keys to your happiness.

Freud's generation was one of sexual repression and fear of eroticism. Today the conditions are reversed. Our society is extremely open and perhaps overemphasizes the importance of sex. Both situations can cause problems. A repressed sexuality is clearly not healthy and may lead to neurosis, yet the fierce sexual competition of today's world can cause just as much anxiety. Relationships should be about love and feelings as well as sex.

The truth is that everyone has varying degrees of sexual desire. Freud's era would have been a difficult time for highly sexed individuals living within a repressive society. Today someone who may not require persistent sexual gratification may find the demand put upon them difficult to cope with. Neither situation is right or wrong. Each of us has to find a way that suits us best and not give in to the demands of a repressive or permissive society.

# SEX AND MYSTICISM

*"Asceticism for its own sake is not the ideal of this Yoga, but self-control in the vital and right order in the material are a very important part of it—and even an ascetic discipline is better for our purpose than a loose absence of true control. Mastery of the material implies in it the right and careful utilization of things and also a self-control in their use. Forceful suppression (fasting also comes under the head) stands on the same level as free indulgence; in both cases, the desire remains: in the one it is fed by indulgence, in the other it lies latent and exasperated by suppression."*

SRI AUROBINDO

The mystical explanation for the human sexual condition is that each of us has a degree of life force that is focused in areas of the body called the chakras. The chakras are spiritual energy centers that run up the spine and correspond to different physical, emotional, mental, and spiritual conditions. Someone who is primarily focused on the first of these centers, at the base of the spine, will have a strong spiritual connection with the body. The person may be athletic or have a very sexual nature, or the person may be very emotional and also seek power and domination.

Each of us has energy focused on all seven vital chakras, but the degree of energy dedicated to each one will vary from individual to individual. The base chakra is concerned with sexuality, however, if the life force is focused more prominently on the next chakra (sacral center) on the spinal cord, the person may be energetic and active. If it is on the solar plexus center, the person may be creative, and if it is connected to the heart center, the person will be filled with sensitive feelings. Life force focused on the throat chakra results in a communicative person. If the energy is centered primarily on the forehead, the person will be intuitive; if on the top of the head, the person will have a spiritual nature.

This is an oversimplification of this mystic tradition, but it illustrates the fact that our energy is distributed unevenly. It explains why some people are highly sexually motivated whereas others are inspired by other emotional and spiritual needs. It all depends which chakra that a person is spiritually connected to.

A person's sexual desires also change with age. During youth the energy in the body is low, but it may become oriented around the "higher" chakras as life teaches a person to become more spiritual. Some people may continue to have energy focused on the root center but in addition will have large amounts of energy connected with the crown center at the top of the head. They would therefore be both sexual and spiritual. We are all a unique mixture of spiritual qualities mixed from the palette of the different chakras.

Spiritual energy that is expressed remains vital and full of life. However, if it is blocked, it may stagnate and cause psychological or physical problems. Many people today believe that the blocking of this life force may be the cause of illness and may employ techniques to help this energy flow more freely. For example, one of the primary functions of acupuncture is to help the life force (called chi by the Chinese) flow through the body. The needles of the acupuncturist are inserted in key points to help the chi flow along the spiritual channels, which they call the "meridians."

Spiritual energy that is blocked may cause problems. If a person is focused on the chakras for the heart or head they may have difficulties if the energies associated with these chakras are inhibited. They may experience illness or psychological difficulties if they cannot express their creativity, their feelings, their ideas, or their spiritual inclinations. If the energies that express these qualities are blocked or repressed, the spirit will rebel, and unhappiness and sickness will be the result. Emotional, mental, and spiritual repression are just as devastating to the psychology of the individual as sexual repression. In short, the energies of each person are organized differently.

Some people experience inner conflicts if they reject the sexual side of their nature, but for a healthy life it is essential that the spiritual and physical aspects of life find a common ground. The middle path is best. Sexual over-indulgence and spiritual asceticism are both false paths to happiness. However, the teachings of yoga and tantra (a form of sexual yoga) explain that the life force must endeavor to rise to the upper chakras. A person's spiritual duty is to transform sexual energy into spiritual energy. Celibacy is not the objective of tantra; it is to teach that love is sexuality that has been enlarged, enlightened, and transformed. It could be argued that the real tragedy of the modern age is the lack of understanding that the life force of the body is not destined only for pleasure but also can be used to awaken faculties that permit creative, psychic, and spiritual work. Masters of spiritual alchemy know how to transform the lead of raw sexuality into the gold of pure love.

## Inducing Sexual Dreams

The mystic's sexual path is not for everyone. Because of this, some people are naturally very highly sexed and will enjoy and perhaps encourage erotic dreams. Dreams can be "incubated" to produce specific images and fantasies and these can be an expression of what Freud called "wish fulfillment," which simply means dreaming of something you consciously or unconsciously desire. For example, a person without a sex partner may dream of being intimate with a favorite film star (or writer of fantasy dream books). Some psychologists encourage people to have these sexual fantasy dreams, which are the ultimate form of safe sex!

Psychologists can tell when a person is dreaming because they observe that the subject has rapid eye movements from side to side beneath the lids. This was first noticed during the 1950s and was called REM sleep (Rapid Eye Movement). During REM sleep, dreams take place and the dreamer's eyes dart in various directions corresponding to the type of action taking place in the dream. During sleep, REM sleep normally occurs every 90 minutes, and the average sleeper has four or five REM periods a night. These periods last about 10 minutes at the beginning of the sleep cycle and extend to between 30 and 45 minutes in the early morning. It is not unusual for men to have erections during REM dream states and for women's vaginal areas to moisten.

Dreams clearly have a physiological connection with the sexual functions of the body. From a spiritual point of view, it can be explained that sexual dreams help keep people in touch with the first chakra, the sexual center, which is important to the maintenance of all the others. This chakra connects us to the earth and our human nature.

## DREAM INCUBATION

The dreaming mind can, to some extent, be influenced by your thoughts as you fall asleep. Repeating a command to yourself as you "drop off" influences the subconscious to produce dreams according to your commands. In effect you are programming the biological computer that we call the brain. Dream incubation can be used to solve specific emotional, creative, and practical problems. It can also be used to induce sexual dream fantasies.

The simplest way to encourage an emotionally satisfying sexual dream is to apply simple dream incubation techniques. Spiritual practitioners sometimes use this method to link the chakras and harmonize the sexual and spiritual sides of themselves.

To induce dreams you will need to spend a little time relaxing before you go to sleep.

**Step 1:** As you lie comfortably in bed let your breath slow down and allow yourself to enter a state of complete relaxation.

**Step 2:** Once this is achieved, imagine a brilliant light shining from your first chakra at the base of the spine and linking to another brilliant light at the crown of the head. In kundalini yoga these are the two primal spiritual energy lights of heaven and earth, male and female, body and soul. Visualize these two primal energies merging together and becoming one.

**Step 3:** As you sink into a deep enjoyable sleep, issue a command to your subconscious mind: "Tonight show me the highest meaning of love and sex. Let me dream of becoming one with my ultimate partner."

**Step 4:** As you continue to voice this command inwardly, imagine yourself in a place you remember, a beautiful place that gives you great joy. It may be a scene from nature that you see from a holiday or a beautiful place from your imagination.

**Step 5:** Repeat the command a number of times, and allow yourself to gradually slip into sleep. Now let go and allow yourself to think as normal. Your subconscious mind will continue with the instructions as you sleep.

**Step 6:** Any dreams you have about a lover resulting from this incubation will likely represent the highest aspect of physical and emotional love. Any such dreams will likely inspire you toward greater emotional and psychological integration. As well as being an enjoyable experience, these dreams can also help you increase your love for others and can be used to work out sexual difficulties.

## The Meaning of Dreams and Fantasies

So, what do sexual dreams mean? Clearly many are simply about the release of sexual tension or the fulfillment of natural sexual urges, but sexual dreams can also say a lot about our hidden feelings and about the motivation that drives us. Sex is more emotionally and physically exposing than any other human activity. You're never more vulnerable than when you're lying naked with someone. Sex reveals you without the protection of your clothes and presents you in a compromising way that you would certainly hide from the gaze of strangers. In dreams, sex and nakedness can be symbols for those areas where people may feel emotionally vulnerable.

DREAM THEMES

### NAKED DREAMS

Supposing you dream about being only partially dressed, for example, forgetting to wear your trousers or skirt to work. You may dream of being in the public eye and being exposed in some way, such as directing the traffic or speaking at a public event while naked or partly clothed. I often get letters to my newspaper columns about this. A schoolteacher wrote to say: "I dreamed I was walking through the school grounds when suddenly I sensed that all eyes were upon me. Then to my horror, I discovered I was wearing nothing but my blouse and underwear. I was mortified with shock!"

Dreams about finding yourself in public and being either nude or partly dressed may express feelings of guilt or inferiority. In the instance of the teacher, it was probably because she was a newly employed teacher and felt the resistance of other staff members to her appointment. Her dream expressed these feelings of susceptibility. At work she appeared self-confident and in control of the situation but clearly the innuendo and undercurrents were beginning to get to her. She was frightened that her weaknesses would be exposed.

Dreams such as these are metaphors that expose the dreamer's perceived faults or feelings as well as sometimes indicating a fear of relationships or of showing your true feelings.

Sigmund Freud once said that his favorite dream was of being naked in a crowd of strangers. He theorized that an unconscious, infantile longing for the free, unclothed moments of early childhood inspired these dreams. Freud would also interpret these dreams as a desire for exhibitionism or wish-fulfillment. However, a more modern approach would perhaps interpret the dream as symbolic of a need for one's life to be more open. In the example of the schoolteacher, she was concerned about being exposed. I have also received letters from people who had similar dreams but enjoyed the experience or who observed that other people in the dream had not noticed anything amiss.

The interpretation of dreams depends largely on the interpreter and his view of life. For one person, nakedness may represent a sexual

DREAMING OF BEING NAKED

situation. For another, it may show emotional vulnerability; and for another, it may show the freedom of the human spirit. If we start off with a hypothesis that "all dreams are sexual," it is very easy by juggling the symbols to adapt any dream to fit our pre-conception. An open-minded dream interpreter will see that the symbols of dreams can have many layers of meaning. For example, one dreamer may dream about a sword as a phallic symbol, and another may see it as an expression of power, and another may see it as a symbol of justice. Clearly, some dream symbols are sexual but others are not.

So a dream of being naked may sometimes have nothing to do with sex. It can reveal something about a person's secretiveness in every aspect of life. It may express both a wish and a need. In some cases the dream may reveal the causes of shyness or blushing; it may be telling you that embarrassment is not something to worry about, particularly if nobody notices that you are naked.

Dreams about being naked may connote honesty and may express sleepers' desires to reveal themselves as they really are. The tone and content of a dream offers important clues to its meaning. Dreaming about being naked at an office party may mean you feel exposed at work. Perhaps something you have done secretly is about to be exposed. You may be frightened that your clandestine plotting will be exposed. Disapproving onlookers may signal guilt, whereas indifferent looks may indicate that something you are concerned about is not really that important.

A dream of being a disgusted onlooker as you look at the nudity of another person may suggest anxiety or an aversion to discovering the naked truth about a person, a situation or even about yourself. Acceptance of the nudity of others indicates that you are aware of the hidden motivations of other people but retain a non-judgmental acceptance. In some cases onlookers clearly approve of the dreamer, and this may show that you feel proud of an achievement (or perhaps a sexual conquest) you have made. Nudity can also have spiritual connotations; it is an expression of beauty and divinity. Ancient goddesses, such as Venus, the goddess of love, Diana, the goddess of the hunt, or the three Muses, who inspire artists, are all usually depicted nude.

DREAM THEMES

## GUILTY FEELINGS AND... PAST REGRETS

Many people feel guilty about having sexual dreams or fantasies. Sometimes the images they see or the dreams they have may shock and upset them. But sexual dreams and fantasies are nothing to be ashamed of, no matter what they are about. They are expressions of erotic thoughts and not necessarily wish fulfillment.

It is not necessary to live out your sexual fantasies. You may play out some ideas in the bedroom, but many are best left in the realm of the imagination. If you lived out all your fantasies you would probably be arrested, but of course, they would no longer be fantasies.

Fantasy can add variety to life, but it is unhealthy to get sexual highs from only one idea or method. Psychologists consider a person to be "fixated" if recurrent fantasies lead to obsessive sexual behavior. This usually begins at a young age, and the fixation can center around a specific person, image, or scene so that sexual pleasure is exclusively associated with it. In these cases sexual fulfillment becomes difficult without the presence of the fantasy.

Nonetheless, it is fulfilling to let your erotic feelings express themselves in fantasies or appear spontaneously in dreams. Sometimes they may express other feelings too. For example a man who fantasizes about rape may harbor feelings of anger toward the opposite sex. Similarly a woman who fantasizes about being raped may secretly desire to be less authoritative in her life. Dreams and fantasies about being tied up may reveal a desire to be more submissive in your day to day life. Probably everyone has heard or read stories about judges and politicians found in compromising situations. A figure of authority who likes to be tied up and spanked by someone dressed as a schoolteacher, for example, may secretly wish to be free of power and influence. The sexual fantasy helps relieve the burden of authority for a short while (and at the same time gives fodder to the tabloid press when the events are found out!).

"I don't do guilt," says the Devil to Arnold Schwarzenegger in the film *End of Days*, yet guilt is a very destructive force. Guilt works in a clandestine way, undermines self-esteem, and eventually destroys a person. Natural pleasures can be spoiled and relationships undermined by guilt. Some people believe that to fantasize about another person while making love to their partner is a betrayal—a sort of mental adultery. They may worry that this is a sign that they no longer love their partner or may be bored with the relationship.

The truth is that fantasy can enhance a relationship and is not a betrayal of the other person. Sexual fantasies are likely to be more intense if you are turned on by your partner, and some couples enjoy incorporating their fantasies into their lovemaking.

Many people feel guilty if they have a sexually charged dream. Your erotic dream experiences are not something that should cause shame; erotic dreams are natural occurrences, and everybody has them. It would be foolish to censor these spontaneous experiences or shroud them in guilt. Remember that, like everything else in dreams, these experiences have a symbolic basis. It is true that they may often be a form of release of sexual and emotional tension; however dreams of incest or promiscuity, for example, may be symbolic of aspects of yourself that are appearing in erotic form. Dreams can use extreme sexual situations and exaggerated sexuality to bring to your attention the emotional undertones that you may associate with these conditions. They need not cause undue worry about sexuality but can be used to give insight into emotional concerns that are bothersome.

Erotic dreams can also express emotional worries from the distant past. The controversial Freudian psychoanalyst Melanie Klein, for example, believed that many of our emotional and sexual problems arise at the early stages of infantile development. Melanie was the only sibling who was not breastfed by her mother. She had a wet nurse. In her work she stressed that powerful raw emotions of rage, envy, and hatred were often present in children, and that paramount to the future emotional growth of the child was the earliest relationship of all—to the mother's breast.

She theorized that feelings of love and gratitude arise in a baby as a response to mother love. "The power of love—which is the manifestation of the forces which tend to preserve life—is there in the baby as well as the destructive impulses, and finds its first fundamental expression in the baby's attachment to his mother's breast, which develops into love for her as a person. My psychoanalytic work has convinced me that when, in the baby's mind, the conflicts between love and hate arise and the fears of losing the loved one become active, a very important step is made in development. These feelings of guilt and distress now enter as a new element into the emotion of love. They become an inherent part of love, and influence it profoundly both in quality and quantity."

The reasons a person may feel guilty about sexual fantasies and dreams are many, but in most cases these attitudes result from repressed thoughts about experiences that occurred in the past. Most people would agree that it is futile to hold onto the past. The present and future are what should be important.

Learn from the past, but never allow it to inhibit your personal growth and happiness. Guilt about sexual activities can be one of the nastiest chains to the past. It is therefore essential to release any guilt carried forward into the present, which can be activated subconsciously every time you have sex. To fully enjoy your current sexual activities it is necessary to forgive yourself your past.

Dreams and fantasies can help with this act of self-forgiveness. They may present you with unresolved emotional issues and give you the opportunity to clear any residue of guilt that remains within you. Whenever the pain of guilt affects you, let it go. Forgive yourself. Allow yourself inner peace. Once you begin this process of freedom from guilt, you will find that your dreams and fantasies will lend you support and provide reinforcing images to help your complete the process of release.

## DREAM THEMES

### SEX WITH STRANGERS

This type of dream may simply be an expression of your sexual feelings. Even though you may be in a loving relationship and be content with your partner, this dream may arise as a natural expression of your sexual desires. Dreams are also a source of great creative potential. Perhaps this dream may give you some insight into the hidden feelings you have and your hidden sexual fantasies.

Dreams can be a pathway to greater pleasure and satisfaction. They can be a way to expand love for others and may show ways to work out sexual difficulties you may be experiencing in your relationship. They can also be very entertaining!

TOUCH OF A STRANGER

Sexual dreams are an expression also of your feelings and your creative energy. In the East it has long been thought that sexual energy can be used for better health and well-being. It could be the basis of what we psychics call the aura. The person overflowing with sexual energy—and who uses it wisely—is in harmony with himself and his partner. Such a person is full of vitality and life, is happy, creative and loves life. Unfortunately, most people either overindulge in shallow sex, which will results in negative energy and debauchery, or suppress it completely and become sour and bad-tempered. Sexual energy that is used wisely is claimed to be the key to a long and healthy life. It is said that Emperor Huang-ti, a Chinese emperor, lived to the age of 300 because he understood the nature of sexual energy when he made love to several women every night.

Sexual energy can be harnessed and used for the health and well-being of the individual. This doesn't mean a person needs to live a hedonistic lifestyle. For example, a person living a celibate life may channel sexual energy in different ways. Many people, including so-called enlightened teachers and religious figures, misunderstand celibacy. Correct celibacy is not a denial or suppression of sexual energy. As Freud clearly demonstrated, this leads only to psychological problems. A master of true celibacy is one who chooses to channel sexual energy in non-sexual ways into other areas of his being. For example, the Eastern yogic system of tantra embraces both the sexual path and the celibate path.

A dream about sex with a stranger may be an expression of your spiritual energy even though it is expressed in a sexual way. Alternatively the dream may represent an expression of basic sexual desire. There's nothing wrong with using sex for pure pleasure. It's okay and natural to dream about sex with strangers; it's not necessarily a reflection of difficulties in your relationship.

Psychologists have noticed that people with potent dream lives are much more self-assured, composed, independent, and competent. Alternatively, insecure people tend to have more symbolic dreams rather than openly sexual ones. Similarly it has been found that people with a high creativity are more likely to have overtly sexual dreams. The dreams of a person of high self-esteem and a high degree of independent thinking are likely to be more sexually explicit than those of a non-creative person.

Some people welcome sexual dreams for their intensity and excitement; others fear them and feel guilt and shame. More than any other type of dream, they always intrigue. In particular, sexual dreams get your attention and seduce you into taking notice of your inner world.

DREAM THEMES

### GAY DREAMS

In many tribal societies sexual ritual is used as an expression of spirituality. Sexual dreams can represent the energies of the psyche. The sexual act becomes a symbol of psychological forces working within the individual. For example, if a heterosexual person has a dream of a sexual encounter with someone of the same sex, it does not necessarily imply homosexual tendencies. The dream is likely to symbolize a desire to attain the qualities of the other individual. Suppose a woman dreams of having sex with another woman. It could be her boss or a strong woman she admires. The dream would likely show that the dreamer wishes to become the boss or to incorporate qualities of female authority into her own character.

Sometimes these dreams represent fears. The threat of homosexual rape may show a repressed homosexual desire; similarly, it could also represent a forbidden desire that needs to be addressed. Forbidden thoughts and desires are not necessarily sexual, but are expressed in dreams as explicitly as possible to get your attention. In any dream scenario in which you feel threatened, you need to ask yourself what it is that the unconscious is trying to force you to consider. Ask yourself if you have problems in your life that you refuse to think about.

Insecurities are also expressed in dreams. A common male dream is of being castrated or noticing they have no penis. The dream may represent actual impotency or, more likely, a fear of loss of control of one's life. The dream may represent a person's fear that there is nothing that the person can do about a situation; the person feels inadequate, feels incapable of dealing with the situation or the emotions being experienced. Again, the things that are upsetting are not necessarily sexual. For example, this dream might occur when a person has lost a job. It could represent the resulting feelings of frailty and powerlessness.

Freud believed that castration anxiety emerged in males as a result of oedipal rivalry with fathers, so called because in Greek mythology, Oedipus makes love to his own mother. Freud believed that boys develop sexual desire for their mothers and feel threatened by the sexual prowess of their fathers. He later termed this incest fantasy the Oedipus Complex. Freud claimed that the fear of castration was a male anxiety but that women can also feel "castrated" and wish to prove that they possess an adequate symbolic substitute for the penis. They consequently feel anxiety toward whatever organ, activity, or object is the penis equivalent for them. Freud called this "penis envy."

Understandably, many women have taken offense at this idea. Nonetheless, just as a man may dream of having no penis, a woman may dream of growing one. My own view is that this is symbolic of the desire for achievement. The penis may represent the traditional male domain of social power.

Homosexuality may reflect a latent, instinctual desire. It may upset a heterosexual person, but is an issue that may need to be addressed. Alternatively, it may express an important need to integrate qualities possessed by someone of the same sex as the dreamer.

## SEX IN PUBLIC PLACES

The setting of a dream that involves sexual encounters may reveal a great deal about its symbolic meaning. For example, if it is set in a school, it may relate to your earliest sexual feelings. If it is set at work, it may show that work takes all your energy or interest. Set in a Victorian house, it may show that you have inhibited attitudes. Set in a hospital, it may show that you are working on healing your sexual anxieties. Any setting can reveal emotional associations you have with regard to your own sexuality.

Dream fantasies sometimes express sexuality in a less inhibited way than normal waking behavior would. For example, you may dream about having sex in a public place. In waking life you are unlikely to give expression to this, but the dream may show a need for sexual excitement in your life. Excitement about getting caught may hearken back to your first sexual encounters, when your parents may have warned you about the dangers of sex. Similarly, it may represent your desire for attention, particularly the recognition and admiration of others.

An unexpressed need for recognition is sometimes expressed in waking life by such deviant behavior as "flashing," obscene phone calls, sexual addiction, and transvestitism. Dreams can act as a safety valve and also help a person understand the reasons for this sort of fantasy and behavior. Getting to the root cause can release the hold it has. I read about a man who had become a Peeping Tom. He enjoyed the thrill of watching women undressing, but his main excitement came from the thrill of getting caught. His therapist discovered that the man's fantasy stemmed from reading pornographic magazines as a boy in the back alley of his home. He was very aroused by them but simultaneously terrified of being caught. As a result, danger and sexual arousal became inextricably linked in his mind. Eventually he was caught. Once the threat of exposure was gone, his interest in voyeurism diminished.

## BONDAGE

Dreams of being tied up may show a secret desire to be more submissive. Someone holding a position of authority in waking life may secretly wish not to have such rigorous control over life and may dream of surrender. Adding a sexual element to this feeling of helplessness increases the intensity and diminishes the stress associated with power and status.

Being tied up may also represent frustration in other areas of life. It may be symbolic of an inability to progress. For example, it may show your feelings about not getting that promotion at work. The addition of a sexual element may add intensity to the dream. If you are naked in the dream, it may indicate your feelings of vulnerability. If you are clothed and your dream partner is bound and naked, it may show a desire for greater power in life in general or in your sexual activities in particular. As with all dreams the symbols can have many levels of meaning.

A dream of bondage may also involve feelings of guilt. You may resist surrendering to your sexual feelings. Spanking may echo childhood experiences when you were spanked by a parent or teacher. Many men and women who enjoy pain and punishment fantasies were beaten, whipped, or spanked as children. The chastisement may have induced sexual arousal, and a link may have been created between punishment and pleasure.

Dreams of sexual bondage may demonstrate an attempt to be in touch with sexuality without accepting responsibility for it.

BONDAGE

## RAPE

Many dreams contain themes of threat. Dreams of being chased typically reflect the response to anxiety that you feel in waking life. Common chase dreams involve being pursued by an attacker intent on harming or killing you. Dreams of being pursued by a rapist usually involve running away, outwitting and out-maneuvering the would-be assailant. Dreams of being pursued by a rapist often end with the dreamer waking up just before being caught or raped. These dreams can be very frightening.

Dreams about the threat of rape are usually about psychological conditions that upset the dreamer. They represent a fear of being united with something. Naturally it may be a fear of sexual intercourse, but the rapist may also symbolize psychological content the dreamer wishes to avoid. The rapist may represent something the dreamer refuses to accept. However, in a forceful way the dream uses sexual union to illustrate that this cannot be rejected, for it is part of you.

Similarly, the anxieties symbolized by the rapist may represent an unpleasant memory that you do not want to think about or a situation in your life now that you are trying to avoid. The intimacy of rape indicates that the material you are avoiding is likely to be very personal and emotionally upsetting.

Freud believed that the human sex drive was the most powerful human experience. He claimed that all energy was sexual and came from the libido, or vital sexual impulse, which sought to find fulfillment in the real world. This raw energy could be controlled or channeled but was not to be allowed to run rampant. If people always did whatever they wanted, there would be no civilization. Freud did not want people to unshackle their sexual energy. He believed that healthy individuals had libidos sublimated into many controlled subroutines that gave them some pleasure, while avoiding going after the things they really wanted. The act of rape showed a libido that was out of control, as did the acts of incest, murder, or stealing.

A libido that has been civilized gives its owner the drive and power to succeed and accomplish great things. However, a wild and rampant libido that devotes all its energy to selfish objectives and that obeys no rules only ruins the owner's life. A dream about raping someone would therefore indicate that the libido has become unruly. It is a warning that the dreamer's desires have become so intense, they are overstepping what is socially acceptable.

Desires revealed in a rape dream may also reflect a desire for power or success as well as a desire for sexual dominance. Someone hell-bent on achieving success on the job may have a dream of raping another person. The dream might express the desire to win no matter what the consequences are. If you are the one being raped it may be a visual expression of "getting screwed." The dream is not sexual but expresses hostility toward you.

In a man's dream, committing a rape may be a straightforward symbol of sexual desire. However, it may reveal sadistic feelings toward the opposite sex or a hidden hatred of women. If you have this dream you would need to ask yourself what it is that makes you want to take revenge. If the dream is about a specific person, you may have a hidden resentment toward the person or the qualities they represent about yourself. Maybe the dream points to something from the past. The dream could be a result of your feelings as a child when your mother appeared to withdraw her love from you when you were a boy.

In a woman's dream, rape may represent unconscious fears of sex. Ask yourself if you have a hidden fear of the sexual act. Rape may satisfy masochistic sexual fantasies.

People who have been raped often have traumatic dreams afterward. The real-life rape is disguised in symbolism and metaphors that represent the way the experience made them feel. Sometimes victims dream of the rape itself, but the details, setting, or characters are often different. Sometimes snippets of the dreamer's past are woven into these dreams.

In subsequent dreams, rape victims dream about other traumas they haven't experienced, such as forest fires and disasters. The terror of these nightmares engenders a common feeling of terror to what was experienced during the rape and helps the dreamer to address the problems using symbolism, metaphor, and allegory. In this way, dreams help the victim to come to terms with the terrible ordeal.

## SOUL MATES AND WHOLENESS

It's the most important question in everyone's life. "Is this the right person for me?" Get it right and you can look forward to a life of happiness. Get it wrong and your world could fall apart. Too many people make hasty or ill-advised decisions about relationships and marriage. Even the professional matchmakers can get it badly wrong. For example, fun-loving Florence, "with eyes of blue, likes a social drink and music," sounded like the perfect match for 23-year-old Andrew, according to the staff at the dating service Andrew paid to join. But Florence turned out to be a 74-year-old retiree. Andrew got his money back.

Perhaps dreams can give you a clue to whom your soul mate is. At a consultation, Sarah S., 24, told me that for years she had had a recurring dream about the same man. "The dream has been with me ever since I was a kid," Sarah said. "I knew every detail about him. His name is Paul. He has dark hair and was in the Navy."

Then Sarah met her dream lover at a club. "Everything about Paul was exactly the same as in my dream," she said. "He was in the Navy and had dark hair, but in the dream he hands me a red rose and a white silk scarf. Paul told me of his recurring dream. In them he hands a woman—who looks exactly like me—a red rose and silk scarf!"

It would appear that Paul and Sarah had been dreaming of each other from an early age. They plan to marry later this year. Some relationships are meant to be, and some people are soul mates. Many people feel that they have a soul mate and that destiny will somehow draw them together. Dreams, they believe, will help them identify this soul mate.

The soul mate idea may also be a representation of the unconscious search for personal wholeness. According to Carl Jung, better relationships happen between individuals who do not look to others to compensate for their own shortcomings. He explained that this type of person brings the diverse aspects of his nature together. One of his early theories was that people fall into two broad psychological categories, defined by their basic attitudes toward the world around them. He called these extroverts and introverts. Extroverts are people who are motivated via relationships and are inspired by other people. Introverts are more reflective, inward-looking, and prefer privacy. Most people are a combination of the two characteristics. Neither is better or worse than the other; they merely reflect a different approach to interaction with the outside world. The extroverted attitude flows outward toward the world and is motivated by external objective factors, whereas introverted energy withdraws from the world and is motivated and orientated by inner, subjective factors.

Jung came to recognize that the terms extrovert and introvert could not explain all human behavior and the theory needed modification. He therefore introduced four "functions" of the psyche, which can themselves be paired into two sets of opposites (thinking/feeling and intuition/sensation). The functions are:

**Thinking:** This is simply the logical assessment of information.

**Sensing:** This involves using the senses to tell what the world around you is like.

**Feeling:** This is the function that uses the emotions to decide whether you like what is going on around you.

**Intuition:** This is your hunches and gut feelings about what is happening behind the scenes.

The four functions are the means by which we orient ourselves to experience. In any individual, one function is conscious and its opposite is unconscious. The remaining two are partly conscious. The functions combine with the two attitude types (extrovert and introvert) to give eight functional types.

This theory casts light on familiar psychological problems. For example, some successful people feel unsatisfied in their jobs, believing something is missing in their lives. This feeling of something missing may arise because success is often an overdevelopment of the thinking and sensing functions at the cost of those of feeling and intuiting. For some people this results in a midlife crisis because of the imbalance in their psyche. According to Jungian theory, the cure for this involves the process of individuation—building up those neglected aspects to bring them into balance with the other more developed ones.

The same applies to relationships. According to Jung, people often seek partners onto whom they project the psychological functions they lack. They look to their partners to make them complete. The snag is that people usually change with time and find that their partners no longer supply the missing parts of their psyche. The result is that the relationship deteriorates and may result in a divorce. Jung advised that the soundest basis for a long-term relationship is for both people to be psychologically whole.

SOUL MATES

# FANTASY FOLKLORE: SEX AND RELATIONSHIPS

*"Probable impossibilities are to be preferred to improbable possibilities."*

ARISTOTLE, *POETICS*

Some of the most enduring fantasies are superstitions, many of which have been with us since antiquity and are cross-cultural. The original meaning of the word "superstition" is "standing still in apprehension or awe." They are believed to be a primitive way of dealing with uncertainty in everyday life. It is therefore not surprising to find that the subjects of relationships and sex have many thousands of superstitions connected to them. Here are few of my favorites:

**Potency:** The Romans had some wonderful ways to increase a man's potency. My personal favorite is the "ointment" of Pliny the Elder. (Please note: Collecting the ingredients can prove a little difficult.) First, you are instructed to rub your genitalia with the urine of a bull that has just mated with a cow. Next, bind to the same part the liver of a frog enclosed in the skin of a crane. Hang the eye-tooth of a crocodile on your arm and then lean your body against the right side of an elephant. The technique is sure to work—as long as you still feel erotic after such an ordeal and the smell of bull urine is an aphrodisiac for the woman of your dreams.

**Fertility:** In parts of America it is believed that if a married couple throws cowpeas across the road near their home the women will become fertile. At Christmas we still hang mistletoe, a pre-Christian tradition. According to folklore, mistletoe in the house protects it from thunder and lightning. It also cures many diseases, is an antidote to poison, and brings good luck and fertility. A woman standing under mistletoe cannot refuse to be kissed by anyone who claims the privilege. Similarly the giving of Easter eggs comes from pagan times as a fertility symbol, and rice, thrown after the wedding ceremony, has always been a symbol of fertility. As you would expect, some of the weirdest superstitions from around the world are about love, sex, and marriage. If you want to meet your soul mate it's important to watch the signs. For example, you may be in for a good time if your lover brings you orchids as a gift. In some parts of England it is believed that this means that he wants to seduce you. Because of their shape, orchids are named after the Greek word *orchis*, meaning "testicles."

**Relationships:** Superstitious young women would use love charms to entrap their ideal mate. The great majority of these love charms that have come down through the ages deal with dreams and how to ensure that the targeted person would visit her as she slept. If she dreamed she saw a man whose face was hidden, it was a sign she would be married very soon but had not met her future husband yet. If she saw a man who was a stranger to her, he was the man she would marry and they would meet quite shortly. Some of the charms to induce these dreams included:

• *Dumb Cake:* Three girls must arrange to sleep together, and the first must borrow a wedding ring from a woman who has worn it for three years. Before retiring, the girls must bake a cake together. The cake must then be divided between them. Each girl then breaks her portion into nine pieces, which they then pass through the wedding ring and eat. The ring is hung above the head of the bed. Not a word may be spoken from the time the batter is first mixed until the last crumb of cake is eaten. Dreams of the future husband will follow. (Naturally I disagree with the cynics who have remarked that this charm is impossible to work, since no three women would keep silent for so long.)

• *St. Agnes Charms:* This one only works on St. Agnes Eve (the evening of January 20th). A young woman must kiss no one during the day—not even a child. She must sleep in a clean nightdress and on clean sheets. She must take nine straight pins and fasten them to the left arm of her nightdress. If she manages to sleep with them all night, she will dream of her future husband.

• *Dead man's love charm*: This Irish love charm is a must for men who want to win the love of a woman. First the difficult part: somehow he must procure a long hair from her head and thread it through a needle. Once this is done, he simply runs it into the leg of a dead man. (It is best if the deceased is a murderer.) The hair has to go to the grave with the body, and as it decays, so love for you will flourish in your true love's heart. Clearly, the simplest solutions are always the best.

**Weddings***:* You would need to invite your analyst to your wedding to fully understand the many hundreds of sexual and fertility symbols that are present in Western wedding ceremonies. However, spare a thought for a Galla tribe bride, of Ethiopia. For good luck and fertility she must, on her wedding day, stiffen her hair with butter and rub her body with civet, which makes her smell like cat urine. The wedding ceremony begins when the bridegroom climbs into the bride's lap and sits there while a mixture of butter and honey is poured over them. Or consider the men of the Macusi Indians in Guyana. To be virile enough, or perhaps henpecked enough, for marriage, they must be sewn up in a hammock full of fire ants. Fortunately, Western superstitions are not quite so painful or messy, but nonetheless we also have some peculiar nuptial superstitions. Many are all that is left of rituals from long ago. Here are just a few from our own fantasy folklore:

• *Sisters and brothers:* It has always been considered unlucky for two sisters to marry two brothers, as there is only so much luck to go around.

• *Birthdays*: It is unlucky to be married on your birthday.

• *Wedding day:* The luckiest month to marry is in June, as it was ruled by the Roman goddess Juno, the faithful wife of Jupiter, who is the protector of women and marriage.

• *Tying the knot:* They actually used to do this in Babylonian times. The priest would take a thread from the bride's and groom's clothes and symbolically tie the couple together.

- *Something blue:* A small blue item with the white dress is a symbol for the sky and the color of the heavens.

- *Bouquet:* Flowers are an ancient symbol for sex and fertility.

- *Omens:* It is bad luck to see a pig, funeral, or be stopped by the police, but it is a good sign if the bride's path is crossed by a black cat, a chimney sweep, or an elephant.

***Modern Superstitions:*** It is believed that blondes are dumb and that when it comes to sex, they are more fun. But before you reach for the bleach, it is also believed that the sexiest people of all are those who have ginger hair. For a man, shoe and hat size are all-important, for men with big feet or a big head are said to have a big penis. Similarly, Latin men and those from hot countries have more sexual potency because of the generative power of the sun. And did you know that many Americans believe that women wearing contact lenses cannot take oral contraceptives, or that a douche with Coca-Cola will prevent pregnancy?

Many people are uncomfortable living in a world of randomness, and superstitions may help them cope. My own work as a medium brings me into contact with many people who are superstitious. Many people believe that burning specially empowered candles will prevent a marriage from breaking apart. One of my clients was told by a "psychic" that her relationship was in danger of splitting. She was advised to buy special magic candles, at $2,000 each. She was told that her case was so bad, she would require at least six! Clearly, as long as there is uncertainly about relationships in people's minds, they will continue to turn to superstition and sometimes fall into the hands of charlatans.

EXERCISE

### DREAMY AND STEAMY

Your sleeping brain is your own biological computer. Program it to work for you using dream incubation. This is a simple technique that should make your dreams a lot tastier.

**Step 1:** Before you go to bed, decide what problem you'd like your dream to solve for you: relationships, work, money, sex...the choice is endless. As this chapter has been about sex and relationships, this would be a good first choice. You have been thinking about these topics, so your unconscious mind is probably already addressing these issues.

Now write down your main problem about relationships in the form of a question. Just before you go to sleep, put it under your pillow. You've just pressed the first button of your inner computer.

**Step 2:** As you fall asleep, run through the issue in your mind. Try to see it in picture form. For example, if you're after a man or a woman, visualize the two of you laughing and chatting together or even having sex, if you wish. Keep the imagery happy; you don't want miserable thoughts.

**Step 3:** Now put the issue out of your mind and let your dreams do the rest. Look forward to your dream. Treat it like a love letter that you look forward to receiving from someone you care about.

**Result:** If you tell yourself you're going to have a dream, you probably will. In the morning write down a detailed account of it. What does the content say about the question you asked? Keep in mind that the dream will give its answer in a symbolic way.

Of course, you can use the same technique for just about anything. Try practicing job interviews or taking exams. You can even visualize being the life and soul of the party and discover ways of becoming the center of attention so no one can resist your charms. Your dreams are like playscapes—use them to do whatever you like. Give yourself an ego-boost by dreaming of being in an extremely successful and glamorous job, or dream that you're the most desirable person in the world when it comes to sex. Doing this will carry the subliminal self-confidence into your waking life and alter your behavior patterns.

## Love and Understanding

Dreams are symbols; don't take them literally. Dreams of dying, for instance, may simply signify new beginnings and change. As an emotional symbol, they may show that you are overwhelmed by the passions and feelings associated with a relationship. Falling may suggest a lack of confidence, and being chased may mean you're running away from a sexual problem. But most dreams don't fit into neat categories. They're unique, and it's how you interpret them that matters. To discover their hidden message, ask yourself:

### "Is the person I dreamt about really me?"

Most of the people you dream of represent aspects of yourself—even the ones you have sex with in a dream! If you dream your lover's too bossy, it may show that you're really the bossy one. Perhaps you're anxious about your own behavior.

### "Does the dream environment represent me?"

For instance, a stormy sea can indicate suppressed emotions, and a barren landscape may express the fact that you feel unloved. What does the landscape say about your relationship with your partner?

### "Can I reverse the dream?"

Try turning the dream on its head. For example, a dream of walking over a carpet with muddy boots may mean you're being walked on by others.

### "Does the dream remind me of an event from my life?"

If it does, try to recall the emotion you felt then and how it may apply to circumstances now. Perhaps the dream holds clues to your feelings.

Use your dreams to alter the way you think. You could be meeting your dream lover in no time, and your dream fantasies might be giving you a few handy pointers to who it is.

# Chapter 3

# MONEY AND CAREER

*"My work is a game, a very serious game."*

M. C. ESCHER

In 1950, an unidentified man walked up to a craps table in the Desert Inn Casino in Las Vegas and played for an hour and twenty minutes. Although he only placed comparatively small bets of $50 per throw, he made his point an astonishing 28 times in succession. The casino calculated the odds against this happening as being ten million to one. If he had been a little braver and had re-bet his entire stake on every throw of the dice, he would probably have won the whole casino.

The chances of becoming a millionaire by gambling are pretty slim, yet many people imagine that one day they may be lucky. Las Vegas and Monte Carlo were built on these fantasies. Similarly, the odds of a substantial win in the lottery are about the

same as being invited to go up in the Space Shuttle.

If a genie were to grant you any wish, most people would ask for millions of dollars. The assumption is that money can buy happiness. This Midas mentality affects most people. Fantasies about being a millionaire suggest a magic formula that money will solve every problem. "If I had a million dollars I would not have to do this dreary job." "If I had a million dollars I would be a more attractive person." "If I had a million dollars I could leave my partner." "If I had a million dollars I could have new friends," and so on...

Money fantasies can be a trap because they prevent you from dealing with the real problems that confront you. Money fantasies are an

DREAMING OF MONEY

"if only" trap. Sometimes it is nice to think about what it would be like to be without material worries, but only as a temporary respite from the tensions of everyday life. People who hold on to money fantasies to such an extent that they spend their days gambling, mugging the rich, or becoming so obsessed with earning money that they place it above everything else, live very deprived lives.

## MONEY DREAMS

*"Every day I get up and look through the Forbes list of the richest people in America. If I'm not there, I go to work."*

ROBERT ORBEN

Dreams about being mega-rich may occur because you are worried about your material situation. The dream may be compensating for the anxieties you have about money, particularly the lack of it. One of the functions of dreams is to help maintain sleep, so dreams like this will help you to forget your worries for a while and give you a change to restore yourself.

The millionaire dream could also be a symbol that warns you about wasting money. For example if you dream you have unlimited spending power and in your dream you spend, spend, spend, the dream might be warning you that you are spending too much in real life. Your conscience might be kicking in to advise you to have a little less "Retail Therapy."

Conversely, the dream could be telling you to be a little less miserly. It may be saying that you should be more generous with yourself and others. It may not necessarily be money that has to be given. The dream could be saying that you are advised to give your feelings a little more readily. You should show people that you care. The million dollars is perhaps a symbol for the psychological qualities that you possess. The dream is telling you that you are rich in spirit.

In the New Testament, Jesus used the parable of the talents of silver to show that people must utilize their own talents in the service of God. He used a clever money pun to demonstrate how you must multiply your qualities and abilities. Your dream may have a similar symbolic meaning. It may show that you are multiplying your good qualities. You are developing as a person. Similarly it may be showing that you are becoming more skilled or creative.

If the dream has a feeling of expectation of becoming a millionaire it may be a metaphor to express something you are aware of in your life that excites you. It could be symbolic of a forthcoming event, such as a promotion or perhaps a birth or marriage. It can be an expression of your anticipation that something good is about to happen in your life.

When you understand what human qualities being a millionaire represents in your fantasy or dream, you can build a fantasy to increase these positive qualities. People who believe themselves to be lucky invariably become more successful than those who forever believe failure lurks around every corner. A positive fantasy about being a millionaire will increase your sense of being a lucky person and give you the self-confidence needed to bring about good fortune in your life.

If you have money worries in real life, fantasize about abundance and see yourself attracting good fortune. Taking an attitude of "success breeds success" and inwardly believing yourself to be fortunate and lucky may actually influence the situations and opportunities that come to you. Gamblers certainly believe in luck. Some researchers and philosophers believe that the mind can directly influence the world. For example, German biologist Paul Kammerer proposed that periods of good or bad luck are not chance occurrences but are meaningful events governed by strange new laws of nature. He believed that luck was controlled by a mysterious force in the universe drawing events together in the same way gravity holds particles of matter together.

If you think lucky, you will draw good luck to yourself. If you are materially challenged, imagine yourself in a situation in which all your material desires have come about. You have a big car, a big house, and a wallet stuffed with platinum credit cards and hundred-dollar bills. Picturing yourself in a situation of success will considerably increase the likelihood of making these things part of your life.

Naturally, you must also be practical and not get carried away spending everything you have. Unfortunately, I've not found a way to spend your way out of debt. However, you could increase the affluence fantasy by dressing in a way that attracts money. An expensive suit or dress will sometimes work wonders by giving you the self-confidence you need to trigger this affluence energy. It also sends out subtle signals to the people you meet. It never ceases to amaze me when people call me sir if I wear a suit yet will only grunt a response if I'm in jeans. Clearly, people can get locked into the fantasy we project.

If you feel that the millionaire dream was about emotional issues rather than material concerns, build a fantasy about being emotionally generous. For starters, you can become a "smile millionaire," giving yourself permission to look happy. By doing this you will be putting into practice the emotional qualities that one interpretation of the dream implies. You are becoming generous in spirit.

Smile when you're driving, when you're with people, on the phone, while cooking and washing up. It's difficult to be down when you're smiling because smiling initiates a more positive state of mind. Smiling and laughter release beneficial chemicals into your system and, more importantly, stimulate a flow of positive energy. Practice smiling in a mirror to begin seeing yourself as a smiling, happy person. Imagine your eyes smiling. This will help relax the muscles around your eyes—an area where tension often resides. Ease away that tension by smiling.

## FINDING TREASURE

*"To know you have enough is to be rich."*

TAO TE CHING

Money is associated with the material world. In a dream it can show power as well as status. Treasure is of course a symbol of wealth but is also associated with spiritual or emotional importance. For example, you might call a child "my little treasure," but would probably not call the child "my little wad of dollar bills." Treasure is closely associated with the things you value. It is something that is kept and protected.

In mythology, treasure is often guarded by a dragon or a demon. It is sought by the hero. These mythical fantasies reflect the psychological symbolism of dreams. The hero bringing back the treasure is a metaphor for bringing up the content of the unconscious. Sometimes castles or caves are guarded in which lies a great treasure. When the guardian is overcome we inherit the castle's fortune, which is in reality the treasure of our own personality. In many of the stories the hero, who represents the conscious self, rescues the maiden, who symbolizes the unconscious female side of the personality. The treasure is obtained because the opposite aspects of the personality can now come together as one.

## Dreams About Treasure

It is very common for a person to dream about finding treasure. This can of course represent material success in your life. You may have recently received a raise or a promotion at work, for example. As with other dreams about wealth, it may represent material gain of some kind, such as buying a new house. Because the sleeping mind sometimes has the power of prophecy, it may also be an insight into a forthcoming improvement in your material circumstances. Similarly finding treasure may represent your expectations that things are soon to get better. It is certainly a dream that brings with it new hope and optimism.

Continuing the literal theme this dream may also show that you are worried about finances.

The optimistic theme of the dream may be telling you that now is a good time to start a new venture. The treasure may also represent feelings of security, independence, or power.

The most likely interpretation of this dream is that it represents uncovering a previously hidden part of yourself. Perhaps there is something that you have neglected or repressed. Is there something about yourself you value very highly but because of circumstances have had to push out of your mind? It could be thoughts about a person you once loved but no longer think about. Similarly the treasure could represent a talent such as an artistic or musical gift that is no longer active within you. Could it be something from your childhood—an old memory that is only now coming to the surface?

The dream may be showing you that there are neglected parts of yourself that are important to become aware of so that you can become whole again. It could be that you have repressed something that is no longer threatening and is now coming into your consciousness again, an aspect of yourself that you undervalued.

## Treasure Affirmation Fantasy

As you can see, treasure represents something about yourself you value. Your first step must be to discover what it is. Your unconscious through your dream is encouraging you to have the faith to rediscover this hidden part of yourself. This could be the time to discover what you really want from life.

A CASTLE CAN SYMBOLIZE WEALTH

In your daytime fantasies you could imagine yourself in a mythical setting in which you are a knight in shining armor rescuing a maiden from the castle and then inheriting its great wealth. Okay, it's a fairy tale, but you are nonetheless using your imagination to help bring yourself to inner wholeness. One of the reasons these stories are so enduring is because they appeal to a part of us that lies below the surface of normal awareness.

If your fantasy involves dragons guarding the treasure, ask yourself what it is that makes the monster so fearful. What is it you fear in life that prevents you from achieving success? Similarly, you may ask what is it about yourself that you fear that stops you from finding psychological wholeness? If you get good at constructing fantasies, you could ask the dragons to speak to you. Imagine asking them the question, "Who are you and what is it you guard? What does this treasure represent about my life and what I need to achieve?" This technique of talking to your fantasy characters is recognized as a therapeutic technique and can give you insight into your fantasy dreams and their meanings.

## EARNING MONEY

*"Not what we have but what we enjoy, constitutes our abundance."*

JOHN PETIT-SENN

Our unconscious fantasies may associate earning money with caring. Earning money enables us to give to the people we love and support—our family and children. This is a fact of life. Below the surface of our consciousness, however, our unconscious fantasies may exaggerate the importance of money. It is no longer just a practical thing to buy things with, and becomes too closely associated with emotional concerns.

## EARNING TOO LITTLE

*"Even though work stops, expenses run on."*

CATO THE ELDER

Dreams and fantasies can help in a positive way to cope with financial difficulties. It would be foolish to ignore the detrimental effects of having too little money, but the emotional impact on the personality can be lessened. Lack of money can seriously undermine a person's feeling of self-worth because it is imagined that everything else of value will be destroyed too. Sometimes the loss of self-esteem can be so bad, a person takes his own life. Developing a positive approach to a period of financial difficulty can lessen its destructive effects and give you the self-confidence to address the problems. Too often, fantasies about money are laden with emotional significance that turn them into symbols of other things.

### Too Little Money

Anxieties about having too little money will be represented in your dreams with symbolism. The worry may be represented by a dark, shadowy figure. Although this type of image may also represent many other things, including aspects of yourself that you have not yet accepted, in dreams worries are given human form. If you refuse to face up to a problem and continually push it out of your awareness, it may appear in a dream as a menacing figure. For example, you may dream of being chased by a dark figure or stalked by a stranger.

Sometimes of course dreams may be about other issues rather than money. A dangerous figure carrying a knife, for example, could show a fear of male sexuality. A frightening character in a dream may have certain qualities associated with money worries. For example, a man wearing a traditional pin-striped suit may symbolize your bank or worries about your bank account. A beggar asking for money may represent the way your life feels at the moment. Similarly you may associate debt with certain familiar people who appear in your dream. A childhood friend whom you borrowed a dollar from and never repaid can stand as a symbol for your present difficulties. Because of the long time associated with this person, it may indicate that your financial troubles have been with you some time too.

Many images that occur in your dream have personal associations. Some reveal long-standing attitudes that have established themselves as bad habits and that prevent you from being more successful. Here are a few common dream themes that may occur if you are thinking about money:

## FINDING YOUR FINANCIAL DIRECTION (SIGNPOSTS AND MAPS)

Maps and direction signs often occur in dreams and can give important indications about how to solve worldly and inner problems. Not all dreams about money are necessarily about material situations. Maps and directions in dreams may be signposts to self-discovery. They point out things about you and your behavior. They can also lead you to the root of what may be causing your emotional upsets.

A signpost may be showing you the direction to take in life. If words are written on the sign, it may hint at the nature of what you should be doing. For example, if a city is shown, it may say something about the situation you are dreaming about. Suppose it said "Rome." This may have many personal associations for the dreamer but one possible pun may bring to mind the saying "Rome wasn't built in a day." What lies down the road will take time to achieve but will be worth it. In the other direction the sign says "Boston." The word could perhaps be a pun on the word boss and express your thoughts about becoming your own boss.

Some of these suggestions may be stretching a point, but dreams really do make quite extraordinary associations sometimes. The theme of wealth and material success may occur in dreams in all sorts of strange guises.

The setting of dreams is often symbolic and significant to the overall meaning. When I ran my own small advertising agency I had a dream of being in Zurich, Switzerland. The town looked wonderful, and I was particularly impressed by the hundreds of fountains I saw everywhere I looked. There was a feeling of pleasant expectation.

I could not understand the dream. However, a few days later I received a telephone call from a Swiss investment company whose head office was based in Zurich. In fact the word "Zurich" was part of the company name. This dream was clearly a prophecy of a very important business contact that proved very important to my business success. The dream was foremost in my mind when I drove to the organization's headquarters. Flanking the driveway on the approach to the main building were six magnificent fountains.

Not only are dreams problem solvers, but they can give access to information there would be no way of knowing otherwise.

You will have personal associations with certain places and cities. A financial center such as New York may represent your material life and financial aspirations. If you work in New York or have direct connections with the city, the symbolism may be more specific. For example, one of my publishers is based in New York, so dreams set there are usually— for me—symbolic of my work as a writer. Many of the ideas I have had for this book are based on dreams set in the Big Apple. Everyone has particular associations with places, cities, and countries. By working with the symbolism, you can gain clues that will help you benefit from specific financial opportunities. The signposts may point you in the direction of material success.

Dreams about maps also give important information from the unconscious that may lead to opportunities. People often talk about "mapping out the future," the "lay of the land," or "plans." Signposts can give ideas for direction and arise spontaneously in the unconscious. Dream maps show strategy and may deal with plans you have already made. Plans that are not quite formulated in your mind may come in the form of notes or letters that you receive in a dream. These are messages from your unconscious mind. Often they tell you about yourself and your emotional situation. Occasionally these notes may give you clues to help you achieve wealth.

From an emotional and psychological standpoint, maps can represent your personal life plan. They may show emotional, intellectual, and spiritual goals as well as material ones. The map may be a representation of you. It may be a symbol for your emotional and intellectual potential and may illustrate your faults and your positive qualities. Sometimes maps may have a mystical quality and represent the course of your life and your potential destiny. Prophetic dreams are often connected with the reading of maps.

Treasure maps may represent your desire to find spiritual insight. Treasure, and particularly gold, can be a symbol for the higher self. However, the treasure may be a literal symbol for your material success. Take note of maps that are shown to you in dreams. They may reveal many important ways for you to find the material or spiritual success you desire.

## WEARING JEWELRY

Dreams about jewelry follow the treasure theme. Jewelry may represent something of value. We wear jewelry to adorn ourselves, so it may symbolize the things that we value about ourselves. If you have dreams centered around this theme consider what personal qualities are represented by the jewelry. What is it you most value about your human qualities? Other themes in the dream may help reveal these things. For example, jewelry worn during a battle may represent your courageous qualities. Jewelry shown in a romantic context may represent your loving qualities. It is also likely that the dream is showing you the qualities you lack and need.

Or the symbolism of jewelry may be telling you not to undervalue yourself. It may be saying that you have the psychological resources you need. You have an inner treasure of abilities and attributes. The truth is that achievement is generally more about what you bring to a situation than about external elements. The symbolism of this dream reveals the qualities you have at your disposal.

Certain jewels have developed a symbolism of their own. Diamonds, for example, because of their durability and perceived value are associated with eternal love. The phrase "diamonds are forever" is evocative of a love that will live eternally, hence diamond engagement rings as a promise of marriage. This theme of an eternal promise occurs in superstitions that claim it is unlucky if an engagement ring has to be altered for any reason, and if the ring should become loose before the wedding then the marriage is not going to be a happy one. It is also unlucky to lose or break an engagement ring.

Rings can also symbolize a promise. Dreaming about a ring may symbolize your emotional life and your relationships. Perhaps you are thinking about your or your partner's loyalty. This dream may have nothing to do with wealth but may be a symbol of fidelity. Similarly, it could symbolize loyalty to your principles and ideals. Also a circle, with no beginning and no end, can represent eternity, wholeness, and your true self.

Many fantasies are associated with jewelry. The jewelry a person wears often reflects the person's personality, and in particular the image the person wishes to project into the world. A man or a woman who wears large, extravagant jewelry may wish to tell the world, "Look at me, I'm rich!" Large, chunky jewelry, such as the gold blocks worn by some men, is considered by many to be in poor taste. It puts quantity before quality and is often worn by those with no real financial status. Artificial jewelry makes a similar statement about a person's status fantasies.

Unfortunately for us men, many women associate jewelry with how much a man desires and cherishes her! There are a great deal of emotional associations connected with jewelry. Often jewelry is given in love, but sometimes it is given in appeasement. Jewelry manufacturers play on these fantasies. An advertisement for a diamond ring is unlikely to say "top quality diamond at a bargain price." Instead you are more likely to buy (or be told to buy!) with a slogan that says "tell her you love her."

Jewelry is also a symbol of protection. In your dreams it may represent a need to protect your vulnerability regarding things about yourself you would prefer to hide from other people. In ancient times jewelry was used in magic amulets and talismans fashioned to combat the dreaded "evil eye." During Celtic times, makers of these "magic stones" began putting them into special settings. They were used as charms against disease and misfortune and fashioned into brooches. Often they bore magical symbols and Latin incantations.

The associations with magic talismans perhaps account for why some jewels have very strange fantasies and superstitions associated with them. For example, the famous 44.5-carat "Hope diamond" was believed to bring misfortune. Supposedly ripped from the forehead of an Indian idol by a wandering French mendicant, the diamond is said to carry a curse. It is claimed that the diamond came into the possession of King Louis XVI of France, who gave it to his wife, Marie Antoinette. They were both beheaded in 1793.

In 1830 the stone was bought by banker Henry Thomas Hope. The Hope family were soon to fall on bad times, as did the others who owned the diamond afterward. Jacques Colet took his own life; Prince Ivan Kanitovitsky was murdered; the Sultan Abdul Hamed of Turkey was dethroned; and Simon Montharides and his family were killed by a shying horse.

In about 1907 the diamond came to America and was purchased by jeweler Pierre Cartier who sold it in 1911 to Mrs. Evalyn Walsh McLean. Her daughter later died from an overdose of sleeping pills, and her son was killed in a car accident. Eventually the stone was given to the Smithsonian Institution, in 1958.

According to a report in the *Washington Post* on August 21, 1959, James Todd, the mailman who delivered the stone to the Smithsonian, was beset by constant bad luck. Within that year, one of Todd's legs was crushed by a truck, he received head injuries in a separate car accident, his wife died of a heart attack, his dog died after strangling on its leash, and four rooms of his house were burned in a fire. When he was asked if he thought his misfortune was connected to the diamond's curse, Todd stoically replied, "I don't believe any of that stuff."

## WEALTH DREAM THEME

### GAMBLING

Many people have fantasies about being lucky as an escape from the banality of their life. Despite the incredible odds against winning a lottery ticket, the fantasy always wins. Often these fantasies are enhanced by superstitions. For example, the six luckiest objects to carry into a casino are said to be: locks of hair, animal bones, "holy" relics, four-leaf clovers, hooves, and coins with a hole through the middle. And of course a beautiful woman attracts great good fortune (and probably costs one, too).

In dreams, gambling may symbolize the fact that you are involved in some kind of risk-taking in ordinary life. It may, of course, be a financial risk but it could equally apply to an emotional risk. People often speak of taking an "emotional gamble." Your dream may reflect worries about your relationship with your partner. For example, a person having an extramarital affair is certainly taking a gamble with future marital security.

Similarly, a new relationship may feel like an emotional risk to you. When you let down your social barriers you may feel emotionally vulnerable and exposed. You are introducing a chance factor into your life over which you have little or no control. This may upset you in some way. The act of gambling often has the desire to escape emotionally as its driving force.

If you dream about losing, it may show that you feel that something has been lost from your life. The dream may reflect a situation in your life, such as the breakup of a relationship, or it may show that you have lost certain human qualities. For example, the dream may be telling you that you are not as loving as you once were or as confident as before. You have lost something of yourself. Perhaps you feel that you have been "lucky in money, but unlucky in love"?

A dream about winning may symbolize the opposite of the above. The dream may reflect success you have had. You may feel you are not deserving of the rewards given to you, that they have come through chance instead of hard work. The dream could represent a legacy or something that has recently come to you. Again the dream may have emotional overtones. In regard to relationships it may be saying that you can't believe your luck, or it

may be pointing out that you should consider how fortunate you really are.

## *BEING ROBBED BY A MUGGER*

Dreams about being robbed may have a literal meaning in that your unconscious has recognized something amiss in your financial affairs. The dream may be drawing to your attention a flaw in your strategy for success. Your financial security is exposed in some way and subject to attack by others. You may want to act on the dream and check the security of your property and the amount of money you carry. Similarly you might want to look at your finances and make sure nothing is amiss. The dream may spot something simple, like an accidental overcharge to an account or an incorrect bank charge, for example. Dreams often use exaggeration to get the attention of the conscious mind.

The dream may also express the way you feel about something that has happened in your working life. Perhaps someone at work was promoted ahead of you and you feel you were robbed of an opportunity. Similarly if you failed an exam, you may feel you were cheated of your success. The dream identifies an opportunity that has been taken away from you.

Being robbed or mugged can also indicate that you have been emotionally hurt in some way. You may feel that a situation in your life has robbed you of your self-esteem, or a relationship gone wrong has robbed you of your self-confidence. Once again, you will see that dreams very often speak about your emotional life and the way you feel about yourself and the conditions of your life.

The emotion of fear is associated with being robbed or mugged. In a way, it shows your vulnerability. You feel threatened by something. The robber or mugger is likely to be a shadow figure, a common dream theme that has been recognized in the work of the psychologist Carl Jung. The shadow can represent the things you fear about yourself, such as your own self-destructive tendencies. Shadow figures may represent something you have repressed. Tendencies that might in some circumstances be able to exert a beneficial influence are transformed into frightening figures or demons when they are repressed. This is why many people are afraid of the unconscious and of spiritual self-exploration.

Some people have exaggerated fears about leaving the house for fear of being mugged. Naturally it is wise in any big city to be aware of potential dangers, but this caution can become unrealistic. This may come because the person is in reality afraid of confronting something personal. Inner fears may prevent the person from facing the world, retreating instead into agoraphobia.

Carl Jung pointed out that although the shadow contains the hidden, repressed, and nefarious aspects of the personality, it is not necessarily always a destructive force. The shadow may contain positive qualities that you do not recognize, such as normal instincts and creative impulses. It is related to the wholeness of the personality, just as thought and feelings are related to each other.

A positive response to dreams and fantasies about being mugged or robbed is to ask yourself what has been taken from you and why it gives you a feeling of fear. You may think about this in a material way, such as the influences current in your work, and so on, but it is worthwhile also to examine the questions from an emotional standpoint, to ascertain what is missing from your personality or being neglected.

## BEING A BEGGAR

Dreams and fantasies about being a beggar are more likely to be about feelings of loss of self-esteem than about financial circumstances. Your prospects at this time may be poor, but the figure in the dream is a symbol of your feelings about yourself and your situation.

The circumstances within the dream are important too. How you react to the beggar may reveal a great deal about your feelings and your situation. If you reject the beggar, it may show that you reject part of yourself. For example, your emotional self may be begging for attention but the conscious you is only interested in material success. Many people in the world today are very successful financially but are spiritually and emotionally no more than beggars.

If you show generosity toward the beggar, it may demonstrate that you are either showing a benevolence of spirit in your life or need to become more giving emotionally. If you are the beggar in the dream and people don't give you money, it may mean you feel as if people are passing you by. You may wish for emotional attention from the people you know or may want to find someone who will give you emotional attention. You feel impoverished spiritually. The beggar image here may show your need to be loved.

## LOSING YOUR PURSE OR WALLET, OR FINDING IT

I have noticed from my work with the bereaved that dreams about the loss of a wallet or purse often occur after the death of a loved one. These dreams are not a prophecy that a death is going to take place but represent the emotional aftermath of losing a loved one. The search acted out in the dream is the search to find what has been lost from the dreamer's life. The wallet or purse represents the shared feelings that were of great value to the dreamer. Often associated with this dream are the feelings of panic and anxiety that accompany the loss of a pivotal person in one's life.

Similarly the dream can relate to an emotional loss, such as occurs at the breakup of a marriage or when a child leaves home. The dream demonstrates your need to regain the feelings that have now gone from your life. It may show your need to reconcile an emotional situation and may encourage you to recognize the need within yourself.

Other anxieties can be shown in this dream. Worry often appears in life when you fear

you will be unable to cope. The dream may represent a component of your life that is missing. It is expressing your worries and uncertainties. Naturally your finances may also be at the heart of this dream. You worry you will be unable to have material control of your life. You will need to address this issue before you can adequately deal with your practical problems. Often people waste time worrying about not having money when the best course of action would be to apply energy to earning money.

## BEING UNABLE/ABLE TO PAY A BILL

Of course this dream may be dealing with your material conditions. The dream may express your fears about loss of status and power. Even when you have an affluent lifestyle there is often the hidden fear that everything will go wrong and your fortune will take a turn for the worse. Many spiritual teachers have pointed out that material things cannot bring happiness because they are transitory. Eventually old age will overtake you. All the money in the world will not save you from your date with death. Happiness can only come when we are centered on the spiritual truths that are within.

In dreams you sometimes wrestle with spiritual issues, even if these things are not part of your conscious life. Why we are here and what the purpose of life is, are recurring themes. The dream may be showing you that money is not everything.

The most likely meaning of dreams of this nature is that you feel worried you will not be able to fulfill your obligations. It could be a disguised sexual dream showing worries about impotence. It can also show your concern about not being able to give what is expected of you emotionally. This dream may also occur if you feel unable to complete an important task or project. Maybe you have an upcoming examination and you don't feel you know enough.

The obligation you are worried about may be in just about any area of your life that causes you concern. Other details in the dream may reveal what it is. Suppose you dreamt of visiting a prostitute and you were unable to pay. This would clearly reflect your sexual fears. Sexual and other themes usually occur in a disguised form or a less obvious way. For example, if you cannot pay for a meal in a restaurant, it may show worries about fulfilling your sexual obligations. Sigmund Freud considered eating to be a symbol of the sexual act, as the mouth is the primary erogenous zone. Again the dream expresses your sexual worries.

Perhaps you feel that the emotional price is too high for some other issue in your life. Suppose your employer demanded that you work in another city and you knew it would entail moving and would disrupt your children's education. Clearly this would be "too high a price to pay."

## Fantasies About Earning Too Little

Many people justify their poverty by creating fantasies to justify their situation. For example, how many parents say to their children, "I work myself to the bone for you," and so on? Most children don't care about money. They become selfish and money-oriented because parents train them to be that

way (with a lot of help from advertising agencies). At Christmas a parent might worry about not being able to afford the number-one toy of the season, yet what children really want is time. Time is the most precious gift you can give anyone.

Negative fantasies about money also keep you from financial success, I believe, by setting up negative energies that influence reality to push away opportunities. Some people are unable to feel that they deserve any money at all for themselves. They devote themselves entirely to the needs and greed of other people in their life. This is particularly common in families or with single parents who through misguided guilt feel they must overcompensate for affection from the missing partner.

This affluence-rejection may result in a permanent state of poverty as a silent response to a belief that everyone else is much richer in all ways. A person with this type of fantasy may fear that by achieving success he will attract envious attacks from others. Money and power walk hand in hand. Some people fear this power. This will naturally prevent them from taking any steps to improve their own financial position.

## Affluence Affirmation Fantasy

You can use dream imagery to reverse your negative fantasies about money. Poverty consciousness probably affects just about everyone in some way. Many people worry about the responsibility of success.

To negate this negative thinking, you need to establish new habits that override the poverty thinking that creates the difficult financial situations. You can't wave a magic wand and simply imagine the problems

PROSPERITY CONSCIOUSNESS

away, but you can create the inner conditions to empower yourself to be more self-confident in money matters and empower yourself to take advantage of opportunities when they present themselves. In addition, you can generate an affluent energy around yourself to attract good fortune.

One of the most interesting fantasies that people have used to create good fortune is the Chinese art of feng shui. I am not saying that feng shui is just fantasy. I actually believe it can work and does influence the energies in an environment. However, part of the success of feng shui is that it corrects the inner environment. We manipulate the outer environment and this sends subtle psychological signals to the unconscious to remind us that we will be successful in health, wealth, and happiness. I believe that this is one of the reasons it can work for us.

The Chinese system uses mysterious Eastern symbols that trigger an unconscious response. According to the ancient Chinese, good luck is not a result of chance but is created by *chi* energy that is all around us. We may think of *chi* as a life force that moves like wind through the environment. It also has the qualities of water, for it absorbs and releases the vibrations given out by the things it comes in contact with. The *chi* around you at this moment may be full of positive influences that will make you lucky, or the *chi* may be filled with stagnant influences that will bring you misfortune. In addition, this *chi* energy can influence your wealth, your health, your relationships, and every aspect of your life. Negative *chi* can harm the quality of your life, but good *chi* will make you healthy and happy.

Feng shui is an excellent way to use the power of positive fantasy to influence your fortune. It is perhaps best to learn a little about it and do DIY feng shui. This is particularly important, I believe, as it has a more marked effect on the inner conditions that lead to success. As an addition to traditional feng shui techniques, include images that arise from your own unconscious. For example, if you have had dreams about treasure, as mentioned earlier, you could hang pictures that remind you of your dream. Similarly, any positive images that your dreams give you can be directly represented or subtly hinted at so the inner feelings of success are magnified.

## EARNING TOO MUCH

*"Your prosperity consciousness is not dependent on money; your flow of money is dependent on your prosperity consciousness. As you can conceive of more, more will come into your life."*

LOUISE HAY

Just as many people fantasize and have dreams about earning more money, those who are well off may have fantasies about the problems associated with having too much money. Jealousy is the reaction of some people if they see a friend succeed. This may disguise itself in many different ways, and these envious feelings may be projected in a number of ways. Money is such a source of power, it can draw envious attacks from others. Because of this, it may cause a person to see his success as being in the way of his happiness. The person may reject success because of this or try to isolate himself from other people by becoming totally independent of others to avoid the pain associated with involvement. Of course this is no solution; it only causes feelings of isolation and rejection.

Very rich people often have many negative fantasies about money. They may find it hard to trust other people for fear that their interest is not in them but in how much they can take from them. There are certainly many people who prey on the rich and famous or project the strangest fantasies onto them. With this level of success comes a natural suspicion of people's motives as well as anxiety that others may want to harm them. John Lennon had a continual fear that someone might try to shoot him. Unfortunately what he thought was a fantasy turned out to be fact.

A person with this sort of fear may have anxiety dreams about being stalked by a shadow figure or may have dreams involving vulnerability, such as being naked in public or exposed in some way. Being rich or overpaid may contribute to feelings of being put on a pedestal. This may in itself cause anxiety, and a rich person's dreams and fantasies may include fears about being defeated or harmed in some way. Sometimes the pressures of riches or fame may make the person want to escape the public eye. If an outlet cannot be found for this fear, an unreasonable course may follow. For example, a successful executive may resign or retire early, because the burden of income or status may be too great.

## Power Dreaming

Most of the time you don't realize you are dreaming until you wake up. But have you ever had a dream that was so vivid, you thought you were wide-awake? These "lucid" dreams are the key to many psychological powers.

If you "wake up" in a dream and realize that you're still asleep you can take control of the dream and make it do whatever you want. Studies have shown that 73 percent of the population have had at least one lucid dream, and it comes naturally to between five and ten percent.

If you learn how to "lucid" dream, you become like a Hollywood director directing your dream as if it were a film. Lucid dreams help you to gain control over your dreams and may also give you greater self-confidence in everyday life. The achievements you make while dreaming can act as a dry run for achieving the same results in your career. The content, characters, and actions within the dream all come under your control.

EXPERIMENT

### POWER DREAM TECHNIQUES

If you want to control your dreams, then there are certain techniques you need to try out.

***Lucid Dreaming:*** During the day, keep asking yourself, "Is this a dream?" Of course it's not, it's everyday life, but it will start a subconscious habit of raising the question. This will help you get into the habit of questioning if you are dreaming. At the same time you ask the question, do something simple, like clapping your hands. If these become regular actions in your daily life, they will find their way into your dreams. And if one day you clap your hands and they pass right through each other, you'll know you're dreaming. Suddenly you are lucid dreaming.

When you go to bed say to yourself out loud six or seven times, "Tonight I WILL wake up in my dream." This will send a command to your unconscious to "wake up" in the dream so that you can manipulate it.

Sound's too simple? Well, this technique really works. At first you may lucid-dream for only a few seconds before falling back into ordinary dreaming, but with persistence you will be able to become aware throughout the dream.

*Lucid Creativity:* Many artists and scientists have used lucid dreams to get ideas from the creative subconscious mind. Lucid dreams can be used to help solve scientific or mathematical problems, paint masterpieces, or even improve a golf game. Wordsworth's greatest poems, he said, were inspired by dreams, as was "Kubla Khan," by Samuel Taylor Coleridge. Jules Verne, Charles Dickens, and Robert Louis Stevenson were all influenced by dreams. And the characters in Jane Eyre were spun from the dreams of Charlotte Brontë.

Dreams can offer creative solutions to seemingly impossible problems. Ideas are the lifeblood of successful people. Your dreams are a rich source of ideas that can be used to enhance your abilities in your career or business. Before you make a major career or business decision, sleep on it. If you make a practice of doing this, you may save yourself from risky ventures and dubious schemes. The fantasies created by dreams will help you see beyond the immediate problems and give you unusual ways of addressing complex issues. Simply becoming aware of the emotional concerns that influence your behavior may help you make more clear-headed judgments in the workplace.

*Use Lucid Dreams to Role-Play!* If you learn how to lucid-dream, you can use dreams to increase your confidence. For example how would you like to be a successful surgeon or a top athlete? What would this do for your self-esteem? In dreams and fantasies you can be whomever you want to be. The difference with lucid dreams is that these fantasies can feel very real indeed. In a lucid dream you may feel that you actually are a great surgeon. Naturally you would not allow this to become self-delusion; but a powerful fantasy like this will show you what is possible. In waking life you may not become the dignitary or respected person of your dreams but you would have tasted what it is like and thereby be able to achieve the maximum within your given circumstances. You have experienced the warm glow of success.

CAREER FANTASY

## Chapter 4

# TRAVEL AND ADVENTURE

*"To travel is to discover that everyone is wrong about other countries."*

ALDOUS HUXLEY

Whenever I sit in the dentist's chair I fantasize about being somewhere else. I often imagine myself walking through the Old City of Jerusalem, one of my favorite places from my travels. I can hear the clatter from the narrow streets, smell the air in the marketplace, fragrant with exotic spices, and see the golden glint of the Dome of the Rock against the skyline. I become completely immersed in the fantasy until the dentist's drill seems far, far away.

Of course, it doesn't always work. There have been times at the dentist when I haven't had time to get involved in my fantasy, and I've sat there and flinched at the slightest pain. "Oh, my God, he's about to use the slow drill—the one feels like

it's screwing you into the floor. Ahhh! Here it comes. Here it comes! Let me out of here!"

I've concluded that it's good to use escapist fantasies in such situations.

Fantasy can be used to escape intolerable pain. For example, some people can perform amazing physical feats, such as piercing their body with skewers or hanging by piano wires threaded through their bones, yet they apparently feel no pain. Some have an unusual physiology that allows them to do these things but others accomplish these feats using only the power of the mind. They imagine they are somewhere else. One stuntman I saw described imagining that he is in a "warm comfortable place a little like a womb where nothing can possibly harm me or hurt me." He then proceeded to do things to his body I won't even begin to describe.

The man used the incredible power of fantasy to allow him to push his body to the limit. Under normal circumstances such pain would be unbearable. Yet he didn't even blink. Asked whether he ever feels pain, he explained that he always feels pain if he has not had time to prepare and put himself in that "special place." If he unexpectedly stubs his toe he will cry out in pain like any normal person. Only when he is immersed in his fantasy of another place can he be free of pain.

Clearly fantasy can be used to help cope with severe pain. Similar techniques have been tried with hypnotism, the first being in 1766 when Antonio Mesmer successfully used hypnotism as a form of anesthesia. The first full operation was conducted by Recamier in 1821. Jules Cloquet followed him in 1829, Dr. John Elliotson in England, Dr. Albert Wheeler in the United States, and the well-known Dr. James Esdaile in India in 1840. Today some clinicians use hypno-anesthesia to prepare patients who can have only moderate use of anesthetics or are nervous about their operation.

To help a patient deal with pain, the hypnotist will suggest that the patient imagine being somewhere else. The hypnotist will help the patient imagine being in a place that is secure and happy, and will encourage the patient to experience the pleasurable sensations that this place provides. Often the place he suggests will be somewhere the patient already knows.

In a similar way, most people use fantasy about other places to escape unpleasant situations. How often have you been at work or in a classroom and fantasized about being somewhere else? When you feel depressed or worried about your situation, you might recall an enjoyable vacation or a place where you felt happy and at ease. These fantasies come naturally and are a safe, temporary escape from the harsh rigors of everyday life.

Dreams use travel and other places in a similar way to help you escape the trials of everyday life. In addition, they use settings as symbols to describe feelings and thereby give insight into problems. Most importantly, fantasies about travel and foreign lands are symbolic of a journey of self-discovery.

Also, by transferring a familiar problem to an unusual dream setting, you are given a new perspective about patterns of behavior that have trapped you. Just as you see your old routines in a new light when you return from a vacation, so too a fantasy dream set in another place can give you a fresh insight into your current concerns.

## DREAMS OF PARADISE AND HELL

*"In all chaos there is a cosmos, in all disorder a secret order."*

CARL JUNG

I have a recurring dream that is set on a wonderful coral island somewhere in the tropics. The place feels completely familiar. Usually I am swimming in warm waters through rocky coves and I can see colorful outlines of coral shimmering beneath me intertwined among weeds flowing like a mermaid's hair. The water is warm and crystal clear. I can hear the gentle rustle of the viridian green foliage, and the occasional squawk of an exotic bird cuts through the quiet. The island smells fresh and alive.

When I awaken from this dream I feel inspired and at peace.

Dream fantasies about paradise have a naturally restorative effect on the sleeper. These dreams put you in touch with a part of yourself that transcends the problems of ordinary life and connects you with a state of spiritual perfection. It may also be your dream's way of giving you a temporary respite from your troubles. In some instances it may represent your desire to return to the innocent problem-free simplicity of early childhood.

Fantasies about paradise occur in mythologies from around the world. Usually the symbolism points to the perfection of the human spirit and primal innocence when humanity was at one with God. In particular, think of the Garden of Eden, in the Book of Genesis. Psychologist Carl Jung pointed out that paradise is a symbol for the human spirit, and this place may often occur in dreams to indicate the integration of the spiritual aspects of the self. However the "dark side" of the ego is also often present in these dreams. This is the aspect of the human condition that Jung called the "shadow," and it includes sex and survival instincts. It derives from our pre-human, animal past, when our concerns were limited to survival and reproduction, and when we weren't self-conscious.

In Eden, the snake symbolizes the "dark side" of the ego, the evil we are capable of. The shadow is amoral, neither good nor bad, just like animals. An animal acts according to its instincts, but from the human perspective, the animal world looks rather brutal, inhumane. So the shadow becomes something of a garbage can for the parts of ourselves that we can't quite admit to. The shadow is what we discard and fear about ourselves. It is the snake in paradise.

Jung points out that the God who created Eden also created the snake and so intended us to taste of the fruits that give us the desire to have knowledge and free will. Similarly the shadow self that appears in dreams should not be feared, for it may bring self-knowledge.

Continuing the Jungian interpretation of the symbolism of Eden, the garden represents the oneness and harmony of all things when all things were still unconscious. This can represent the individual's innocent state as well as humanity's before it became conscious. Similarly it can illustrate the loss we face when we leave our mother's womb at the start of this life. With the advent of conscious thinking arises critical thought and the agonizing choices that come with free will, represented in the Genesis story by the eating of the fruit of the tree of knowledge.

A dream about Eden may represent your desire to avoid conscious choice and return to the primal innocence. However there are many layers of meaning to this story and to

GARDEN OF EDEN

associated dreams. According to the biblical story, Adam and Eve were expelled from paradise to prevent them from eating from the tree of life, which would have given them immortality. The tale really concerns the process by which we enter earthly life and live out our mortal lives. Your dream may be asking metaphysical questions about your own mortality.

Dreams about hell as the opposite of paradise may symbolize your inner troubles and your feelings that you have lost control of your situation. Your dream may simply be saying, "My life feels like hell at the moment," and may be an expression of the emotions you are feeling or trying to push out of your mind. The paradise dream shows the opposite. It represents a time when you feel in harmony with yourself or shows what it would be like to be in harmony with yourself. It is a symbol of personal wholeness.

Hell-like places may also depict the frightening aspect of the unconscious. When you first discover this other side of yourself it can appear fearsome and overwhelming. You are no longer who you thought you were. You now face a dark chasm of things you don't know about yourself. The fires of hell may represent the emotional forces that threaten to engulf you. They may also say something about angry feelings you have or the passions or repressed instincts and emotions.

Hell may contain everything you've shut away. However, in order to attain personal wholeness, represented in dreams by the ascent to paradise, you need to face up to the repressed contents of the unconscious and tame them by transforming their negative energy into something positive.

---

## DREAMSCAPES

*"If you want to understand the jungle, you can't be content just to sail back and forth near the shore. You've got to get into it, no matter how strange and frightening it might seem."*

CARL JUNG

The landscapes you see in your dreams and the fantasies frequently symbolize inexpressible moods. The light, the weather and the features of the landscape all say something about the feelings you associate with your dream. For example, a gloomy landscape set in an ominous twilight may express feelings of depression or worries about a problem that is looming. It may show that the clarity of the daytime consciousness is dimmed as the "Inner Nature" reveals itself in its own light. Light is a common symbol of consciousness, so a sunny landscape will represent the fact that you are aware. Moonlight, however, may represent the intuition and the feminine, unconscious aspects of yourself. To see the sun dawning shows the first steps to spiritual illumination and is often a symbol for rebirth and hope.

The nature of the weather in a dream also expresses the way you are feeling. When you are depressed, you are "under a cloud." Expressions such as a "stormy argument," "saving for a rainy day," or even a "sunny smile" attest to the fact that weather conditions can be reflective of emotional states. The

SUNNY DREAMSCAPE

weather in your dream landscape most likely represents your state of mind.

Many dreams give warnings about inner conflicts or about the things you fear or dare not express in waking life. Bad weather as a backdrop to your dream landscape may indicate that you feel there are troubles ahead. Dark clouds and wintry weather may express a feeling of lack of emotional warmth in your waking life. Stormy skies may show arguments and anger, whereas sunshine may indicate feelings of happiness. Rain falling after an oppressive period can show release from tension. The dream may give clues about how to remove the causes of tension in your life. Perhaps there is even a message of hope—symbolized by a rainbow.

The structure of the landscapes also reflects your feelings about the dream content. A landscape that is hard to travel over may show that you feel that there are many emotional or practical obstacles in your life. If the dream is about your love life, a rough landscape may show the hindrances that prevent you from forming a happy relationship. You may feel that there are emotional boulders in the way or perhaps feel that you have been sucked into the quicksand of previous bad attitudes. Perhaps you feel unable to express your feelings and therefore dream about a barren desert scene. Similarly the obstacles in a dream landscape could relate to difficulties you face in any aspect of your life—obstacles at work, in relation to your spiritual development, the need for money, things that are preventing you from being happy, healthy,

and so on. Your dreams create a symbolic scenario to represent what is happening within your outer and inner life.

What you see mapped out before you in your dream may represent the challenges that you know lie ahead of you in real life. For example, mountains in the distance can represent a problem that has to be overcome before you can complete your inner journey or achieve what you want in life. Scaling a mountain can represent your desire to attain higher awareness or to achieve material status. The symbol of climbing will frequently occur in the dreams of someone who is ambitious. The same theme may be expressed by climbing stairs or a ladder. However, these dreams can also contain warnings about an impending fall from grace should your become overconfident or overambitious.

Obstacles in the dream landscape can be an expression of your everyday problems. Trying to cross a busy street, fording a river, climbing a mountain, or attempting to cross a chasm show how you are dealing with your perceived difficulties. These may be material or psychological problems that need to be overcome. For example, the obstacle dream may represent a financial worry or a relationship problem, or the obstacle could be a symbol for an examination, a health problem, or an inner weakness. In waking life these troubles can be dealt with in stories. This is why everyone loves to read about the hero who overcomes insurmountable obstacles, why movies with characters who win despite the odds are so popular. In sports, people often like to see the "little guy" win. These fantasies appease inner fears about the many restrictive hindrances everyone faces in life and reflect many dream themes.

One of the most important aspects of dreams is that they can help with the process of inner growth toward psychological and spiritual wholeness. The landscape of dreams is filled with metaphors that express day-to-day worries but also the highest spiritual aspirations. In particular, the journey of self-discovery goes to hidden places within—to areas of the mind that are unconscious. This undiscovered side of the self also connects you to the world of shared human experiences that Jung called the "collective unconscious."

Below the more recently evolved outer surface of the brain, where activities like logic and language formation are believed to occur, sits an old brain structure called the cerebellum. This area of the brain controls movement and the body's muscles, but it is also believed to be the home of ancient memories from prehistoric times. From the cerebellum arise terrifying images that have been banished from your civilized consciousness. However, in these dark places lurk the monsters from an earlier, more dangerous age. Many of these inner fears date back to the dawn of human consciousness.

The dark woodland is a common symbol for your journey through this unconscious part of yourself. The woods can represent the primitive side of your nature and may connect you to ancient symbols and behaviors. For example some psychologists believe that dreams of falling date back to when we lived in trees and sometimes fell to the jungle floor. The memories of falling have been passed to us through generations. We never hit the

ground when we dream of falling because these dreams come from the memories of our primitive ancestors who survived the fall. The others died and therefore did not pass on the genes for this memory. (This is just speculation, as we have no clinical evidence to prove that memory can be inherited.)

Fantasies that occur in ancient myths are a creative expression of our relationship with the unconscious. They are the secret opening through which inspiration can find expression. Dreams spontaneously boil up from this same primordial world of myth.

One of the most appealing mythic fantasies of the modern era is fond in the books the *Hobbit* and *Lord of the Rings*, by J. R. R. Tolkien. The story is a classic journey of the hero in search of himself. In particular, we are taken into the mysterious Mirk Wood—a symbol for the unconscious—and discover all sorts of strange people and treasures. This story has such an addictive appeal for so many people because it is in effect telling the story of the search for personal identity though the unconscious. Similarly, the fantasy of *Wind in the Willows*, by Kenneth Grahame, uses the dark forest as a symbol for inner exploration. Again in the darkness of the woods we find wisdom, in this instance it is in the guise of Badger. Grahame and Tolkien were probably unaware of what they were doing, but they were unconsciously using archetypal landscapes that have occurred in storytelling throughout the ages. From an analytical psychologist's point of view, these stories are an expression of an individual's journey through unconsciousness to awareness and integration.

Dreams about the jungle may also connect you to your ancient past. The wild inhabitants are probably neglected, disorderly, and maybe mutinous, instinctive drives and emotions. Sometimes the things you discover in the jungle or wood are your repressed feelings, such as guilt, anxiety, and insecurity. And of course the dream may have a much more down-to-earth meaning. It could be speaking about how you "cannot see the forest for the trees," that you are overcomplicating your problems and need an overview. The dream may indicate that you feel trapped in a situation that is hard to escape from. Sometimes city life is referred to as a jungle.

Animals in the forest may represent instinctive drives and emotions. In myth they are often tamed by the conscious self. For example the god Orpheus charms the beasts with his song, and Jesus is represented as the Good Shepherd. Both parallel the archetype of the devotion and piety of the man of nature.

The journey into the unconscious may also be symbolized by going underground. This type of journey metaphor is clearly speaking about what lies below normal, conscious awareness. The descent into the underworld also has a positive aspect. This is a journey of discovery into the unknown part of you. In the darkness of this netherworld you can discover your unconscious true self. This symbolism may also be a representation of the womb. Entering the underworld may sym-

bolize regression. The imagery includes the hope of rebirth.

Journeying under the ocean can also symbolize this exploration of the unconscious that occurs in dreams and fantasies. A dream about a boat journey may show that you are ready to explore the intuitive and instinctive aspects of yourself. Putting out to sea may represent this journey into the unknown part of you.

Clearly, the womb symbolism is even more apparent here and this type of dream has been claimed to represent a desire to return to the security of your mother's womb. It may represent your own mother or Mother Nature. A follower of Freud would probably say that to dream of drowning in the sea may represent a fear of being suffocated by a dominating mother or mother attachment. Exploration of the sea bed may also represent the exploration of the hidden part of you.

The sea can represent the feminine, such as intuition or receptiveness. The moods of the sea may express the way you are feeling at the moment. A stormy sea may indicate that you feel angry about something or threatened by forces outside of your control. A calm sea may represent inner harmony and peace of mind.

## FOREIGN COUNTRIES AND CITIES

*"Still round the corner there may wait,
A new road or a secret gate."*

J . R . R .  T O L K I E N

I have never been to Russia, yet I quite often dream about this country. It could be something to do with a past life perhaps, but as this is a country that is unknown to me, it may represent the unknown within myself. My dream journey to this place represents my explorations of the unconscious. As Russia is a cold place, these dreams may be about my emotional life and perhaps the need sometimes to express my feelings. Unless they have specific personal associations, cold countries represent the need for warmer feelings in your life.

Similarly, hot places can represent passion. You may associate Italy and France with love and romance. A dream set there may symbolize the romantic side of you. Alternatively, you may associate art with these countries and they may represent the need within you to find expression for your creative urges. Your dreams will find many ways to use landscape to express your feelings or make comments about your life. If you are worried about your tax bill, you may set your dream in a tax haven such as Switzerland or the Cayman Islands; if it is about your instincts, you may set the dream in darkest Africa.

Often dreams will use the symbolism of countries in a stereotypical way but will also draw upon your personal associations. For example, if as a child you became separated from your parents and lost while vacationing in Florida, you may dream about the same area in adulthood as a symbol to show the way you feel emotionally lost now. Dreaming about being lost in a strange place is a common dream theme. You may dream of being lost in an unknown city or even in the jungle.

Dreams about being lost are one of the most common themes I receive letters about in response to the dream columns I write for newspapers in the United Kingdom. These letters often express the feelings people have when they break up a relationship. The dream shows that they feel emotionally lost because their life lacks purpose and, as the dream shows, has no direction. Similar dreams occur if someone loses a job or at times when life becomes so banal, it seems meaningless. In particular this sort of dream will happen if a person has neglected his inner life at the expense of the material. Dreams show you how to find sustainable inner happiness that is not dependent on externals.

Dreams about being lost are often accompanied by other anxieties. You may dream you are late for a meeting, or you may not be able to catch a taxi, or perhaps you miss the bus or train. These dreams focus on running out of time and missing opportunities. Perhaps you need to allow yourself more time to complete a project. Perhaps you secretly desire not to reach your goal, that you are of two minds about something. The dream may relate to a specific problem that is worrying you or a more general theme, such as a feelings about having "missed the bus" in relation to life generally. Maybe you need to rethink your direction and the purpose of your life.

Dreams set in the city may represent your practical concerns such as your work, goals, and ambitions. However, a city can also represent the totality of you as a person. Psychologist Carl Jung pointed out that cities are frequently a symbol for the self. In particular he noted that in dreams the structure of a city is often symmetrical and forms a mandala. (Mandala is a Sanskrit word for "magic circle" and is used in the East for meditation purposes. Mandalas are characterized by a circle, which radiates from a central point.) Jung interpreted mandalas as an expression of the fullness of the self and wholeness, symbolized here by a symmetrical cityscape.

A number of ancient and medieval cities were indeed built in a symmetrical mandala shape. Paris and Rome have streets built around a central point with roads radiating outward in a mandala form. Many ancient sites were built on a circular grid. The city of Atlantis and the Heavenly City of Jerusalem (in the book of Revelation) were supposedly built like mandalas and may say more about the perfection of the human spirit than about utopian society. According to Jung, every building and townscape that is mapped to a mandala format is an expression of the human desire for wholeness and is a link to ancient aspirations. Jung wrote: "Such things cannot be thought up but must grow again from the forgotten depths if they are to express the deepest insights of consciousness and the loftiest intuitions of the spirit, thus amalgamating the uniqueness of present-day consciousness with the age-old past of humanity."

In dreams many of these ancient symbols occur spontaneously to represent your spiritual growth and your assimilation of the unconscious part of yourself. The journey through the mandala represents the struggle toward spiritual perfection. Some people spend their lives traveling in the hope of finding happiness, but perhaps they have taken the wrong path, for the place they seek is not in a foreign land but within themselves.

# STRANGE BUILDINGS

*"If a man is created, as the legends say, in the image of the gods, his buildings are done in the image of his own mind and institutions."*

LEWIS MUMFORD

Your inner dream journeys will bring you to many strange places where you will encounter unusual buildings. These are also symbols that express your inner state.

Houses in dreams are usually metaphors for yourself and sometimes for your own body. The upstairs usually represents consciousness and the higher self, while the basement symbolizes the subconscious. Buildings that are under construction may represent projects you are working on, such as your spiritual and mental development or plans you are making. Similarly buildings in a state of decay may symbolize your negative feelings about your self-image, bad health, or may represent aspects of you that have been neglected.

The upper part of the house is associated with the head and the part of the mind where rational thinking takes place. To dream of going upward in an elevator may show that you are raising your awareness. This could also represent your ambitions, for we associate "up" with success and "down" with failure. It could even be a pun for getting a "raise."

The upper part of a building represents the things you are aware of, whereas dreams about the basement show the aspects about yourself that are still unconscious. The basement and attic are places where people tend to store the things they no longer use. Dreams about these places may show those parts of yourself you have either neglected or no longer believe to be important. But sometimes among this junk you find something valuable; perhaps you have talents from the past that could be of value today.

The size and structure of your dream house also says something about you. If it is cramped this may show your frustration. Perhaps there is a part of you that needs expression or perhaps things within you need integrating into consciousness. The cramped environment may indicate that you are repressing your instincts and emotions. Clearly you need to allow this aspect of yourself a little space in your life. Castles and prisons also feature in many people's dreams. They can represent feelings of frustration but may also be aspects of yourself not given expression. For example, a beautiful maiden imprisoned in a castle may show the feminine side of a man that he needs to integrate into himself. Similarly, the heroic prince can show the male side of the personality of a female dreamer. Castles are often shown as a symbol of unconscious contents that remain locked away from the conscious self.

Many people have fantasies about having a bigger and better home. Often a person will fantasize about having a bigger and better home to compensate for their feelings of frustration. A bigger home is lovely to have, but it does not bring contentment. Perhaps it is not a bigger home you need but a more expansive inner life.

I often have a dream about a huge house that, as in the story of Gormenghast, by Mervyn Peake, appears to go on forever. In this intriguing place are thousands of rooms and all sorts of strange environments. There are sections that resemble Rome and others that are like a Victorian theater. In some places the walls are carved into Chinese sculptures, and there are areas of endless corridors hung with magnificent paintings. Ceilings are decorated with the constellations from the zodiac. Some areas of the house are in pristine condition and others have fallen into decay. I believe that this house represents my inner life. My exploration of its many areas is symbolic of the exploration of myself and maybe even of some of my past lives. The modern areas represent my conscious ego and the oldest, the deep layers of my unconscious, what Jung called the "collective unconscious."

Houses and buildings in your dreams can help you discover so much about yourself and your life. Often the buildings are symbolic of specific aspects of your life. For example, you may dream about your paternal home. What you feel in this dream may say a lot about your childhood feelings and about your attitude toward your parents. Similarly, a dream about your work environment may reveal things about your secret ambitions and shortcomings.

Buildings may also represent the body. A decaying building may show aspects of yourself that are being neglected, but the dream may also reveal worries about your self-image as you grow older. You may feel just like that grandiose old building that has seen better days!

The ancient Greek Hippocratic Oath is a code of conduct that is still sworn by doctors today and ensures the confidentiality of a patient's records. The modern version has changed from the original, but the first oath charged that physicians should study the dreams of their patients as these could reveal the cause and cure for many illnesses. As buildings in dreams often symbolize the human body, they are a rich source for medical diagnosis. For example, it is common for a person with a full bladder to dream about being on a toilet. The dream tries to integrate the bodily discomfort into the dream in order to maintain sleep. Eventually you wake up, get up, and run to the bathroom.

There is probably very little symbolic significance to such a dream, but it does show that the dreaming mind is aware of the body during sleep and creates scenarios to represent the bodily condition. Suppose you dream of a house with broken plumbing. Couldn't this be symbolic of a potential problem with the bladder? Broken wiring may symbolize a nervous complaint, and a house infected by rats may show the onset of a disease such as a flu. Similarly, a dream set in a hospital may show the need for emotional or physical healing. The ancient Greeks believed that dreams not only gave a diagnosis but could also suggest the cure for an ailment.

## THE INNER ADVENTURE

*"All human beings are also dream beings. Dreaming ties all mankind together."*

JACK KEROUAC

The call to adventure in a dream is the prelude to the exploration of the unconscious. This is a theme that has been expressed in myth and legend throughout the ages and reflects the need to discover one's true identity. Although in dreams and mythical fantasies it is symbolized by an outward journey, it is in fact an inner journey to the center of existence. The lonely journey brings us into contact with the very heartbeat of the world's consciousness.

The quest for identity is expressed in mythic fantasies and dreams about the journey and quest of the hero. Stories about the hero are one of the most common themes in the classical mythology of Greece and Rome, and the stories continue through the Middle Ages, in the Far East, and among contemporary tribal societies. From society to society these myths have a striking similarity. He usually has a humble birth but during childhood displays special powers that mark him as someone with a special purpose in life. He rapidly rises to prominence and power and undergoes a triumphant struggle with the powers of evil. Eventually he falls victim to the sin of pride (hubris) and his fall through betrayal or a heroic sacrifice results in his death.

For the individual, these stories reflect the process of discovering and asserting the personality, and for society at large, they show the need for a collective identity.

The hero symbolizes a person's unconscious self. His goal is to find the treasure, the princess, the ring, the elixir of life, the golden fleece, and so on. These are all metaphors for one's true feelings and unique potential. In the process of becoming whole, the heroic task is to become aware of the unconscious contents of the personality instead of being overwhelmed by them. The result of this quest is the release of energy and abilities hitherto unable to express themselves.

Joseph Campbell, in *The Hero with a Thousand Faces*, explains that the ancient hero myths reflect the human struggle for identity. The theme reflects the collective goals of all humanity to find meaning and purpose. Today we have lost this objective, and the hero myth has fallen into disuse. Science and technology have externalized our inner life, and the communication between consciousness and the unconscious is lost. Nonetheless the fantasy of the hero myth will continue to manifest but now in a modern guise. For example, the stories about Superman and other superheroes follow a similar format as the classic myths. In the guise of Clark Kent, the hero is an ordinary person just like us, yet secretly he has magical powers. We are the same. We live an ordinary life, yet in the hidden world of the unconscious is the potential to become superhuman. Dreams and fantasies about heroes show that an ordinary person holds hidden extraordinary power. These powers awaken when we rediscover the full potential of the human psyche.

In mythical stories, the hero undertakes an arduous journey in order to find the treasure or release the trapped maiden. He often travels by ship or fights a sea monster. For example, he may, like Jonah, in the Bible, be swallowed by a monster, showing that he has been overwhelmed by unconscious contents. From a Freudian perspective this may show that the person is motivated by an unconscious desire to return to the security of the womb. Escaping from the whale may show leaving the mother, the source of life, behind him, yet experiencing a rebirth.

The hero's quest will take him through a dangerous landscape where he will face his fears in the form of mythical animals and beings. He may discover an Aladdin's Cave of jewels or a dangerous genie. These dreams and fantasies are often accompanied by feelings of fear and dread because they threaten the security most people have built for themselves and their family. They are dangerous dreams, yet the hero knows that the realm he is entering and the adventures he will face carry the keys to unlock the way to discover his true self.

En route to individuation (a term used by Jung to mean self-realization) the hero must resist a number of temptations and challenges. The first figure he may meet on the road to self-realization is his own shadow (another term used by Jung to represent the dark side of the individual—everything you don't like about yourself). The shadow is the side of yourself that has been disowned; it may appear as an evil or frightening figure. It may be an unsavory aspect of your personality that you refuse to accept. In life we imagine that everyone else has the terrible qualities that our shadow represents—everyone except ourselves, of course. Perhaps you have seen other people do this. For example, a terribly jealous sort of person may accuse other people of being jealous. Similarly, a selfish person may accuse others of not giving of themselves. Everyone does this to some extent, and it happens on a collective level too. White people may blame the troubles of the world on black people, and vice versa. Some people identify a particular religious group as the cause of all their troubles. Other people become the scapegoats for our own failings and for everything that is wrong with us and with society. We project onto them our shadow.

The hero's quest is to discover that the shadow figure that appears in dreams is, in fact, the qualities that he has rejected in himself. The process of integration requires him (and each of us) to take responsibility for his faults and stop projecting his shadow onto other people.

The hero also learns to accept the shadow qualities in himself. Negative qualities must be faced and brought to the light if they are to be disarmed. The process of integration that results from the inner adventure requires him to accept these qualities and transform them, thereby helping himself become a more self-aware and full individual. The hero learns to discard the mask of who he thinks he is and, in so doing, becomes the person he really is.

## THE JOURNEY TO THE SELF

*"It is good to have an end to journey towards, but it is the journey that matters, in the end."*

Ursula Le Guin

For both sexes, the inner journey and its challenges are an expression through dream fantasy of the discovery of the true self. Ancient mythical fantasies about journeys, such as those of Odysseus, Hercules, Menelaus, Sinbad, or so many others, are symbols of the inner quest to find spiritual wholeness. The journey symbolizes the search for the inner treasure, represented in literature by wealth or knowledge. At the heart of these stories is the search for, and sometimes the flight from, one's self.

On the second stage of the inner journey is what Jung called the "soul image." These dream "soul mates" are the opposite part of oneself. For a man, the "woman of my dreams" is the female part of himself, what Jung called the *anima*. For a woman, "Mr. Perfect" is in fact the masculine side of her own self. Jung called this the *animus*.

The inner journey to fullness charges you to integrate the opposite side of the personality into yourself. A man must realize and take possession of his feminine qualities, and a woman must recognize her masculine qualities. The anima in a man would therefore represent the inner qualities of receptivity, nurturing, patience, gentleness, and tenderness. The animus in a woman would represent the inner qualities of will power, assertiveness, power, control, and so on. By bringing the

DISCOVERING THE INNER WOMAN

two halves of the self together, the complete human being will emerge. No longer would the man fear being too feminine, or the woman too boyish. Both aspects of the inner life can now find expression. After all, what is the spirit? Is it male or female? In existence, humans are both. People may take incarnations in both forms over many lifetimes on earth.

Dreams about the journey to wholeness include the anima or animus figures. They are likely to appear as a guide who leads you into the unconscious and out again. In many mythical fantasies the male hero is guided by a beautiful female. For example, in Greek mythology Theseus was given a golden thread by the beautiful Ariadne that he could unwind to find his way through the labyrinth in order to kill the minotaur. Psychologically, the labyrinth represents the unconscious, and the minotaur is the threatening aspect of whatever has been rejected within yourself. It is a creature that has gone wild, is unruly, and been imprisoned in the unconscious part of yourself. To kill the monster, the hero needs the masculine qualities of force and discipline but also the feminine quality of love. That is, the hero needs to accept through love this rejected part of himself and welcome it into the light of consciousness.

Dreams help accomplish this integration of the feminine or masculine aspects of personality. The fantastic stories from Greek mythology and other traditions reflect this eternal quest to become a whole human being. The "soul-image" is a mediator that establishes a link between the conscious mind and the hidden aspects that remain unconscious. Also, the soul-image has qualities that are the opposite of those that you project to the world. (Jung called this the "persona.")

For example, if your self-image is an intellectual one, your soul-image may be characterized by the qualities of emotion and sentiment. Similarly, if you are sentimental in real life, your soul-image may appear with intellectual qualities. The anima and animus are figures that show qualities that you lack but will benefit by letting become a part of yourself.

In dreams, the soul-image will appear in many symbolic ways. In a man's dream it may be the "damsel in distress," a mother figure, a sister, or objects with female associations, such as a cat, a womblike cave, or a ship. A woman may dream of a handsome man, a prince, a brother, or an object with male associations such as a bull, stallion, or phallic symbols such as a sword or tower. This male and female imagery indicates that your journey has brought you to a point where the opposite qualities to the one you have need to be recognized as important to your spiritual progress.

Just as you project the "shadow" onto other people to take the blame for your own faults, so you may also project this idealized male or female figure onto the people you meet as partners. This is particularly true if you don't recognize the male or female qualities in yourself. You may project the qualities onto another person and idealize the person. An emotional man may choose a bossy woman, and a strong-willed woman may seek out a sensitive man. These relationships sometimes end in disaster, but recognizing the deficiencies in yourself and integrating the necessary qualities will help you become a more balanced individual. The union of male and female qualities may sometimes be consummated by a sexual dream symbolizing the complete union of the conscious and unconscious, which is the goal of the spiritual journey.

## THE WISE GUIDE

*"A journey of a thousand miles begins with a single step."*

CHINESE PROVERB

Invariably, the hero's quest is initiated by a guiding figure. There is often a guardian working in the background who helps point the hero in the right direction to enable him to perform the superhuman tasks required of him. For example, among the Greek heroes, Perseus had the help of the goddess Athena, Achilles had the counsel of the wise centaur Chiron, and Theseus had Poseidon, the god of the sea.

These figures are symbolic representations of the fullness of the identity that supplies the power the personal ego lacks. The heroic journey often occurs in dreams, when the conscious mind needs assistance with a task it cannot accomplish unaided. The aid often comes from the unconscious mind, which creates symbols and spiritual mentors to guide the individual to a state of fullness of self. It is as if part of you already knows the spiritual goals in your life and the potential you have. I am particularly fascinated by the conscience. Everyone has it to a greater or lesser degree, and its values appear to be universal. All you need do is listen to the voice of your conscience and apply its advice and you will always walk with certainty through this life. It is as if part of you already knows, like the wise guides that appear in your dreams.

Carl Jung called these guiding figures "mana" personalities (a Melanesian word meaning "holiness" or "the divine"). Teachers and sages who appear in dreams and fantasies are embodiments of the wisdom of the ages. Many people project their unconscious fantasies about the wise guide onto others. Instead of exploring this inner source of wisdom, some people choose to disown it and see it as the property of someone else. You might associate the mana personality with a mysterious Eastern guru or with the Pope of Rome, whose dictates are the touchstone of authority for millions. Sometimes the image is seen in a politician, a psychiatrist, astrologer, or psychic consultant.

Jung warns that the mana figure in dreams can be dangerous if it is allowed to take over the personality. I have seen this happen to my colleagues who work—as I do—as mediums or psychic consultants. I have seen some develop wonderful ESP powers, and they have attracted a following of admirers. Problems occur if this adoration goes to their heads and they wrongly believe they are some sort of supermen or great gurus. Jung would say that they have been taken over by the fantasy of being the archetype of the Wise Old Man. They now believe they are filled with infallible superior insight. What once stood as an example of superb mediumship or clairvoyance invariably degenerates into "psychobabble" and sanctimonious self-congratulation. The modesty that comes with true wisdom flies out the window.

Similarly, the negative aspect of the mana personality may be present in a woman who allows her consciousness to be engulfed in the image of the Great Mother. She may fantasize that she is destined to protect and nurture the whole world. These fantasies commonly result in megalomania—delusions of grandeur and power.

In dreams, the mana personality represents your higher self and the innate wisdom within you. It may take a religious form such as Buddha, Shiva, or a saint. The inner guide may also appear as a bearded old man, a priest, prophet, magician, or king. In its feminine manifestation, it may appear as the Earth Mother or a goddess. Because of the awe-inspiring knowledge and insight these figures represent, they may sometimes appear as frightening or domineering people. Dreams of this nature indicate that an extremely important spiritual aspect of your life is opening.

The journey of the hero will bring the dreamer face to face with these strange figures that will act as a catalyst for the dreamer's spiritual growth and insight. As these powers begin to unfold within the personality, the right course is neither to project it onto another nor suppress it. Instead it must become integrated into the personality, as this will enrich you by bringing the intuitive wisdom that comes directly from the unconscious. If a humble attitude is maintained, the conscious and unconscious will be able to work in harmony, becoming complementary parts of the whole. The tragedy of many heroes is that they fall victim to their own self-confidence.

## THE GOAL OF THE JOURNEY

*"Life is a bridge; enjoy while crossing, but don't build a castle upon it."*

UPANISHADS

It is unlikely that your dreams will follow the exact same format I have described in relation to the hero myth and the symbolism of adventures and journeys. However you may sometimes have hints or snippets of this type of dream as the need arises in your life. If you are consciously embarking on a course of spiritual development in your life, your dreams may reflect this journey of self-discovery. The goal of the hero fantasy is to attain self-realization, but as you have already seen there are many potential pitfalls that may keep you from this goal. To have full spiritual knowledge, you must go beyond fantasy; you must experience the truth of reality and yourself. Dream fantasy can help as a symbolic framework to help you toward the direct realization of truth.

The hero myth is a symbol for the emergence of the individual consciousness as it finds autonomy. It is like the child growing to become an independent, self-confident adult. As the new personality unfolds, it discovers the pitfalls and benefits of the unconscious side of the psyche. To dream of a hero myth does not ensure that spiritual liberation has taken or will take place, but it does offer the promise that the individual ego can achieve full consciousness.

Jung said that few people reach the last stage of the process of individuation, though that is the goal of the great spiritual journey.

He called that stage "self-realization," meaning the completion of the whole individuation process, the point at which the ego (the conscious mind) merges with the self (the totality of the integrated psyche). In this state, the conflicting aspects of the individual are united. For example, the extroverted and introverted aspects of the self come into balance. Similarly, what was once unconscious now joins with the conscious, and the two aspects work as one.

The final stages of the great adventure are accompanied by many dream images that suggest death and rebirth. The ignorance dies as the new realization awakens. Many of these symbols have their counterparts in mythology and ritual. Typical metaphors that may occur in dreams are the birth of a divine child, meeting a holy being, the union of a couple in marriage, or a figure with both male and female characteristics. Similarly, you may experience death and resurrection analogies, such as a kiss that awakens a corpse, the dawn of the sun, visiting churches and temples, arising from the sea or earth, or a snake shedding its skin. These are all symbols for the awakening of your consciousness and the unity with your true self. In particular these dreams may be accompanied by mandalas—showing the totality and harmony of the psyche.

The heroic journey may have enabled a specific problem to be overcome or it may have led the seeker to a full understanding of the meaning of that person's life. Instead of thinking and fantasizing, the mind now has the direct knowledge of reality that was formerly the property of the unconscious alone. Your being is whole.

In mysticism, self-realization is attained when the individual awareness merges with the greater awareness of the divine. The self continues to exist but is now part of the One. It becomes like salt dissolved in water. The individual grains are gone but the salt is still there, and we can taste it. Jung's *self* has been understood to mean the fullness of the individuation process but without the loss of the individual self. The realization is that *your* consciousness is also the consciousness that is everywhere and in all things.

The adventures of the hero and the mystical inner journey I have described above are primarily ideas of Carl Jung and the school of analytical psychology. However it is unlikely that your dreams will conform exactly to these structures. During therapy, clients' dreams are influenced by the beliefs of their therapists. Clients of a Jungian psychologist will have mythical dreams, whereas the dreams of a patient with a Freudian analyst will be filled with sexual imagery. It is best to draw from the different schools of thought and work with your dreams in the way that most suits you. All dreams are unique, and the best person to interpret them is you.

Jung's greatest discovery, I believe, was that the goal of the journey is not the denial of life or the subjugation of the self, but an exploration of the fullness of the psyche. This leads to the expansion of the human potential and the direct realization of oneness with the cosmos. Many people consider Jung's teachings closer to mysticism than science, and some even claim Jung helped heal many of the spiritual dilemmas faced by modern man, by building a bridge between science and metaphysics.

## Chapter 5

# CHILDHOOD AND FAMILY

*Our birth is but a sleep and a forgetting*
*The soul that rises with us, our life's star*
*Hath had elsewhere its setting,*
*And cometh from afar:*
*Not in entire forgetfulness,*
*And not in utter nakedness.*
*But trailing clouds of glory do we come*
*From God, who is our home.*

WILLIAM WORDSWORTH

What sort of person would you be today if your family had been different? Suppose you had come from a different ethnic background? Would this have changed your view of the world or yourself? And what if either or both of your parents had died when you were a baby and you were raised by a single parent or foster parents? Would you have been a better or worse person with other paternal influ-

ences in your life? Even your brothers, sisters and grandparents—or absence of them—have contributed to your psychological growth. The truth is, family influences have had a huge effect on your life. They have helped you become the person you are today.

Many of your dreams and fantasies reflect your childhood experiences and your relationship with your parents, grandparents, and siblings. In dreams, family members appear as symbols for the psychological processes that are happening at a hidden level of your being. Influences from childhood work in the background of your consciousness and motivate you in many surprising ways.

For children, fantasy is an important part of life. The stories children are told and the games they play influence their spiritual, emotional, and mental growth. In play, children expand their understanding of themselves and others, their knowledge of the physical world, and their ability to communicate with peers and adults. They explore material and imaginary worlds and their relationship to them. Through the fantasy of play, children learn and develop as individuals and as members of society.

Play is usually fun but also may sometimes include serious reflection. Play is a way of learning that helps develop an approach to action. Exploration is also a key aspect of a great deal of play fantasy. Through play and through a process of curiosity and creativity, a child tests out all kinds of assumptions and ideas about themselves, other people, and the world. Adults, too, gain much understanding of the world through play. Play is the means by which the psyche can unfold.

Many of the games that children play reflect the psychological processes that are unfolding within as their awareness of themselves and the world expands. Distressing experiences a child has had may manifest themselves in play. A child who has been sexually abused may tell a teddy bear things that the child wouldn't dare tell an adult. Psychologists and sociologists recognize the importance of play in the development of the personality and that it can reveal the potential and stumbling blocks a child is encountering.

Play can therefore be used as a form of therapy to help guide children to develop positive qualities.

The fantasies you act out in play express many things about yourself. Could it be that some childhood fantasies express ideas that come from a time before your birth? Could it be that some children's fantasies have their source in previous lives? Many people believe that much of their emotional troubles are the result of unconscious memories brought forward from traumatic past lives. In *Memories, Dreams, Reflections*, Jung wrote that, as a boy, he remembered in great detail being a very old man in the eighteenth century. My wife and I have the same birthmark on the backs of our necks. We believe it corresponds to a death in a previous lifetime we shared together. When we first met, we were astonished to discover we had both had a recurring dream of being attacked by soldiers from behind and having our necks cut through with swords. When our daughter Danielle was born she also had the same marking on the back of her neck. (In recent years my marking has faded.)

A personal friend of mine who is a well-known regression therapist told me that she has met children who are quite certain they have lived before. She spoke of a five-year-old child who surrounded herself with all her teddy bears and dolls. "Are these your children?" my friend asked. The child looked at her with a face filled with indignation and answered: "No, they are my orphans!"

Children have strange fantasies. You have

to wonder what the source of this information is. Cases are on record of children who have been able to speak a language they could not possibly have learned—the term for this is xenoglossy—or have described places that they could not know about.

Some of the most interesting studies were done by Dr. Ian Stevenson, who wrote on the subject of reincarnation. He found cases of children who acted as if they had been transferred without warning from an adult's body into a baby's. "When one of our Turkish children began to speak," he explained in an interview, "almost the first thing he said was, 'What am I doing here? I was at the port.' Later on he described details in the life of a dockworker who had fallen asleep in the hold of a ship. A heavy oil drum had fallen on him and killed him instantly. Cases like this remind me of a woman who had a stroke while playing bridge. When she came around several days later, her first words were, 'What's trumps?'"

It is believed that longer intervals between lifetimes mean fewer memories. For most people, the interval between death and rebirth is long, but occasionally people return to earthly life instantaneously. Children who remember their past lives may be those who have reincarnated quickly. The fantasies that these children display in their play may reflect the traumatic experiences that caused the immediate incarnation.

Stevenson also points out that many children remember being a person of the opposite sex in their previous life. Of 100 cases in which the child recollects having been the opposite sex in a previous life, in 66 of them, girls remember previous male lives. More girls remember boys' lives than the reverse. This gender-changing raises interesting questions about homosexuality and gender confusion. Dr Stevens explains in the same interview: "A biological explanation, such as Klinefelter's syndrome (a genetic condition in which a male is born with an extra X, or female, chromosome) can explain some but not all cases. Western psychiatrists and psychologists do not have a satisfactory explanation for this, whereas in Southeast Asian cultures, gender-identity confusion is considered one result of reincarnation and taken calmly. Reincarnation ought to be considered as a possible explanation at least some of the time."

# FREUD AND CHILDHOOD FANTASY

*"It would be one of the greatest triumphs of humanity, one of the most tangible liberations from the constraints of nature to which mankind is subject, if we could succeed in raising the responsible act of procreating children to the level of a deliberate and intentional activity and in freeing it from its entanglement with the necessary satisfaction of a natural need."*

SIGMUND FREUD

Many people still find Sigmund Freud's theories shocking. Freud presented revolutionary ideas about sexuality, and in particular about childhood sexuality. His interest in sex was not that of the Victorian moralist

CHILDHOOD FANTASIES

keen to judge and preach, but as a scientist endeavoring to analyze and understand. Freud pushed aside the prudish Victorian pre-occupation with sexual morality and claimed that sexual repression and guilt were bad for mental and emotional health. To this day, many of his ideas arouse passionate hostility, especially his views on child sexuality.

Freud believed that children had sexual impulses from the moment they were born. Freud's theories about infantile sexuality claimed that a child comes into the world as a fully sexualized being and attaches himself to his mother in something like the way a man and woman become attached in later life. (Freud is thinking of male children; he had very little time for female children.)

Freud believed that children's sexual urges were a desire to release mental energy. At first the infants gain this release and derive their pleasure through the act of sucking. Freud called this the "oral" stage of development. Gradually the locus of pleasure energy changes as the child grows and derives pleasure from the act of defecation—Freud called this the "anal" stage. Eventually the young child develops an interest in the sexual organs as the site of pleasure (the "phallic" stage) and initially focuses his desires upon his or her parent of the opposite sex with a consequent hatred and envy for the parent of the same sex (the "Oedipus" complex).

According to Freud, children's sexual fantasies about their parent result in feelings of guilt and the recognition that they can never unseat the stronger parent. These fantasies put a boy at risk, for he instinctively knows that in sexually desiring his mother he may be harmed by his father. In particular, the boy may fear that the father may castrate him. Freud called this "castration anxiety."

Fantasies about the desire for the mother and the resulting fear and hatred for the father are repressed and the child usually resolves the conflict of the Oedipus complex at about age five, by coming to identify with the parent of the same sex. At this stage the boy's sexual feelings become much less pronounced. Freud called this the "latency period," which lasts until puberty.

Freud believed that this is the normal way a person develops. It is a process of instinctual drives for pleasure in conflict with parental and social control. Most people resolve these childhood conflicts, but Freud held that unre-solved conflicts experienced in childhood result in mental illness. For example, an obsession with hygiene may result from problems at the anal stage of development; or homosexuality may be a result of a failure to resolve the conflicts of the Oedipus complex, particularly a failure to identify with the par-ent of the same sex.

My own view is that Freud got it wrong. His theories have led people to see children as sexual beings too soon. Children are non-sex-ual but become sexual over time, especially at puberty when they acquire the physical abil-ity to relate to others erotically. Freudian psy-chology tries to undermine this view and in so doing creates a tremendous amount of harm. It could be argued that Freud's ideas are the thoughts of a pedophile.

It has become received wisdom that children are sexual and that their sexual feelings are looking for an outlet, and that these feelings must be channeled in a way that will not cause a disturbance. I wonder whether the explicit sexual education that is taught to children from an early age is necessary or indeed healthy. Today, Freud's views of childhood sexuality seem crude.

There is no real proof of Freud's theories. Nonetheless many parents do notice that children develop a preference for one parent at particular times. A boy may say that when he grows up he wants to marry Mommy and have children. A girl may say she wants to marry Daddy. Some children may have a version of what sexuality is, but few have any concept of the Freudian notion that little boys have sexual feelings for their mothers and have to learn that these fantasies are taboo. If social pressures hold these wild sexual energies in check, surely we would see incest in the animal kingdom, but in nature, where these taboos do not exist, most mammals find their close relatives sexually unattractive.

All the evidence is that a traumatic first three years of life will not destroy a person. The truth is, the things that upset people most, are the ones that happened most recently. Time heals. Research also suggests that even after surviving a dreadful childhood, marrying the right person often saves a person from becoming a complete emotional wreck.

## CHILDHOOD FANTASIES

*"Dedalus and his son Icarus were imprisoned in Crete. The father made them each a pair of wings, and with these they were able to escape. But Dedalus warned his son, "Don't fly too high or the sun will melt the wax on your wings and you will fall. Follow me closely. Do not set your own course." But Icarus became so exhilarated by his ability to fly, he forgot the warning and did follow his own course. He went too high, the wax melted, and he fell into the sea."*

EDWARD EDINGER
*THE MYTH OF ICARUS, AS RETOLD IN EGO AND ARCHETYPE.*

Young children have no difficulty believing in fairies, mermaids, and unicorns. They readily accept that animals and inanimate objects like statues or stones can talk and think like human beings. For a child, there is very little difference between the exterior world and the interior. Both are alive with awareness.

When you respond deeply to a fairy tale, you are being influenced by unconscious forces. The archetypal images stir something in the unconscious part of yourself. The fairy tale, W. H. Auden said, "is a dramatic projection in symbolic images of the life of the psyche." Both Freud and Jung agree that fairy tales and myths do not differ fundamentally from dreams and that they speak the same symbolic language. Favorite stories from childhood can have subtle influences on adult identity.

Many of the themes that appear in fairy tale fantasies have sexual themes—a fact that

Freud was quick to point out and which outraged many of his contemporaries. Many psychologists recommend fairy tales as beneficial to children, believing they help children assimilate problems such as violence, sexuality, becoming an adult, and learning to deal with family difficulties. Violence is perhaps a destructive expression of drives and feelings that are universal in the unconscious mind. In a child's life there may be many conflicts, and fairy tales help the child express the hostility these situations may cause. Fantasy in the form of dreams, daydreams, or fairy tales provides a healthy outlet for socially unacceptable desires.

In real life we teach children not to act on their impulsive desires. They must not hit back or show aggression. However, we teach them—perhaps without realizing it—that it is all right to fantasize about these things. It is acceptable to have these feelings, but it is not always acceptable to act on them.

Fairy tales permit children to destroy the bad parent, often symbolized by a wicked king or an evil stepmother. Sometimes the finger is pointed at the parent without the veneer of symbolism. Would you like to have Hansel and Gretel's mom and dad as your parents?

Fairy tales also moralize and show that hostility toward others is evil. They illustrate that evil destroys or consumes itself. In many fairy tales, the hero or heroine does not punish the evildoer but the villain brings disaster down upon him (or her) self. For example, Snow White's wicked stepmother is consumed with envy in some versions of the story, and she dances herself to death in red-hot shoes at Snow White's wedding. The moral of the story—don't behave violently—also acts as a safety valve for the child's own repressed hostility.

Fairies often appear in stories at times of crisis and preside over the boundaries of life. They may represent figures at the beginning of psychological changes or new awareness. They may be present as a symbol to show crises associated with mortal life, such as birth, adolescence, sexual awakening, marriage, childbirth, old age, and death. In a dream, a fairy may instigate a change. For example, a turning point is achieved for Cinderella when the Fairy Godmother provides her an opportunity to go to the ball. Similarly, the evil fairy in Sleeping Beauty exclaims, "You shall prick your finger on a spindle and die!" Good and bad fairies often act as agents for inner change.

One of the most important functions of fairy tales is to teach the child to use fantasy to help address the problems of growing into adulthood. Perhaps one of the most enduring fantasies is that of the tooth fairy, who visits when a child loses the first tooth. This stage of development is symbolic of leaving babyhood behind. Similarly, stories such as Little Red Riding Hood have sexual undertones. The author, Charles Perrault, shows that being impulsive and giving in to your primitive sexual desire is not the best way to live.

In the beginning of the story, Red Riding Hood is merrily skipping through the forest where she meets the wolf that intends to eat her. Nonetheless, she has a friendly conversation with him. Being innocent regarding the ways of the world, she thinks it is perfectly normal to talk to a dangerous wolf.

BELIEVING IN MYTHICAL ANIMALS

Because Red Riding Hood is young and impressionable, she succumbs to her whim to talk to strangers, not realizing she is informing the wolf of her every move. She is not concerned with what might happen as a result of her irrational choice to speak with a similarly irrational wolf. Clearly, the danger of talking to strangers may also be showing the danger of yielding to sexual desire.

Freud called the primitive unconscious urges the *id* (Latin for "it"). He proposed that there are three structural elements within the mind, which he called *id*, *ego*, and *superego*. The *id* is the part of the mind in which are situated the instinctual sexual drives that require satisfaction. The *superego* is the part that contains the conscience, and the *ego* is the conscious self created by the dynamic tensions and interactions between the *id* and the *superego*.

The Red Riding Hood story shows the task of limiting the blind, pleasure-seeking drives of the *id* by the imposition of restrictive rules. The wolf is also guilty of giving in to his amoral desires. When he first sees the little girl, he "...wanted to eat her but did not dare to because there were woodcutters working nearby." He refrained from giving in to his impulses only because he was afraid of being caught and hurt by the people nearby (the *superego* perhaps).

Eventually the wolf gives in to his desires, heads for grandmother's house, and eats Red Riding Hood. Animalistic desire triumphs. Freud believed that the *id* was the source of all aggression and desire. The wolf represents the essence of the *id*. He relies on his aggression and desire to satiate his wish.

The story also shows the irrational urges of the unconscious. Disguised as the grandmother, the wolf tries to entice the child into bed, saying, "Put the cake and the butter down on the bread-bin and come and lie down with me." His objective is to consume the girl, here a symbol for sexual ravishment. There is no moral judgment for the wolf's part. He is the *id*-driven creature whose only goal in life is to please himself by whatever means necessary. He is unrestrained sexuality.

Many fairy tales have dark undertones. On one level they moralize, but they also express the conflicts happening below the surface of consciousness. In this story both Red Riding Hood and the wolf are guilty of giving in to their *id*. The tale reminds us that in the real world there are wolves that prey on the innocent in order to satisfy their sexual desires, and that everyone is capable of giving into temptation but it is perhaps not the correct thing to do.

Modern children's fantasies express many of the same psychological themes as do those of ancient times. *Star Wars* grips its young audience not only because of the special effects but because it speaks to the unconscious. The themes follow many of the same structures that myths and fairy tales have. The scriptwriters based their plot on Jungian themes. Director George Lucas was greatly influenced by the book *Hero with a Thousand Faces*, by Joseph Campbell, who was one of the greatest authorities on the study of myth. Psychologist and author, Dr. Jonathan Young assisted Joseph Campbell for many years and later became the founding curator of the Joseph Campbell Archives and Library, in Santa Barbara, California.

Classic mythological stories often begin in everyday life, showing the reader that extraordinary things can happen in ordinary circumstances. Tragedy is often the catalyst that sets the story in motion. This is the summons, the call to adventure, the quest, an inner calling from the unconscious.

In the first *Star Wars* movie, the turning point occurs with the devastation of Luke Skywalker's home. This may reflect the circumstances of your own life and may make you look within. For many people, spiritual adventure begins with a tragedy that destroys their familiar world. It might be the death of a parent, a divorce, a devastating illness, or a financial disaster.

In classic myth, allies normally join the hero. In Jungian psychology, this is a representation of psychological energy or spirit. These psychological forces can take many forms, such as an old teacher, a wise old enchantress, or a mysterious old wizard. Similarly, many myths include friendly animals, showing that wisdom comes from nature. *Star Wars* has many strange creatures, including the guiding figure of Yoda, who symbolizes the superior wisdom of the unconscious.

The fantasy expresses a classic hero myth that takes the person to greater self-realization and psychological wholeness. Jung pointed out that one of the dangers to someone embarking on the journey to psychological wholeness is that the person can often fall victim to what he called by the Greek term "hubris." This describes the fate of a person whose "head has become swollen" with powers that are not his personally and which the person mistakenly identifies as personal grandeur, omnipotence, and glory. A classic example is found in the myth of Icarus, who flies too high and whose wax wings melt, plunging him into the ocean. In this case it shows a psychology that has been symbolically swallowed by the unconscious as a result of misused psychological powers. The same theme recurs in *Star Wars* when Darth Vader tempts Luke to the dark side.

Children and adults find the story compelling because it expresses the needs of the individual to become psychologically whole. In the fantasy, the hero achieves the goal of rescuing the princess from the powers of darkness. For a man, this is a metaphor for integration of the female aspect of his own personality.

The mythical heroic man or woman, having done that which seemed impossible, now returns to a level of integration and makes psychological achievements part of his (or her) personality. The task has been enormous. The hero must have assimilated all the best attributes of both genders, must be in tune with the forces of nature, and must have the best allies. At the end there is a celebration and a feeling of fulfillment and achievement. People who undertake the inner quest of the hero become the balanced and focused individuals that typify this concept of wholeness.

The current interest in UFOs may be an expression of this need for wholeness. In 1958, in a book called *A Modern Myth of Things Seen in the Sky*, Jung showed that his theories about archetypes and mandalas explained much of this phenomenon. In his patients, Jung had discovered that the mandala emerged from the unconscious as a sign of the urge toward a new wholeness. The round shape of most UFOs was significant because circles are mandalas. UFO sightings were, in fact, fantasies projected by the modern psyche's need for meaning, showing a mass hunger for wholeness. UFOs, he claimed, were an archetype that would herald a great shift in human history. Something was brewing in the collective unconscious.

figures have had in your life. Often they will be benign figures but sometimes they may take a frightening form as there are still unresolved problems carried forward in your life from childhood.

Here are some of the main figures that are likely to appear in your dreams and an explanation to help you understand their symbolism.

## DREAMS ABOUT CHILDHOOD AND FAMILY

*"The symbolism of my childhood experiences and the violence of the imagery upset me terribly....Who makes me think that God destroys His church in this abominable manner. At last I asked myself whether it was not the devil's doing. For that it must have been God or the devil who spoke and acted in this way I never doubted. I felt sure that it was not myself who had invented these thoughts and images. These were the crucial experiences of my life....I knew that I had to find the answer out of my deepest self, that I was alone before God, and that God alone asked me these terrible things."*

CARL JUNG,
MEMORIES, DREAMS, REFLECTIONS

Naturally the things that have happened during childhood have a marked effect on your life and your mental, emotional, and spiritual development. It is not surprising to find that dreams often draw upon these initial influences that have helped shape your life. Paternal figures will take many forms depending on the emotional influence these

## DREAMS AND FANTASIES ABOUT MOTHERS

*"I married your mother because I wanted children; imagine my disappointment when you came along."*

GROUCHO MARX

We have already covered many Freudian theories about the symbolism of the family. It is unrealistic to assume that a dream about your mother indicates a latent Oedipus complex, and so on. The appearance of these figures in dreams can have a far simpler meaning. The dream may be telling you something about your actual relationship with your mother and your concerns about each other.

A dream about your mother or a mother figure may represent the unconscious, intuitive side of yourself. This may take a positive or a negative form, depending on your attitude to these inner functions. The mother symbol may take many forms. You may dream of a kindly mother, a grandmother, or aunt, or a place, such as a cave, church, or garden. These images may represent the qualities of solicitude, growth, nourishment, and fertility. It may show that certain qualities are arising in your life, such as the development of your intuition or that you are becoming more caring or more in touch with your feelings. Perhaps you are becoming more protective of others who are less able to cope with life, or you may desire to re-experience the feeling of security you knew as a child.

Sometimes the mother image can appear in a negative form. This may show that you have problems with your mother-attachment or that it is so strong that the development of your own individuality has been prevented. The mother symbol may appear as a witch or a dragon and represents dark, destructive tendencies that devour, seduce, or poison. These dreams may be showing that you need to develop a greater degree of inner independence. They may be a stepping stone to greater understanding of your true self.

As well as the dream symbolism described above, many surprising fantasies are associated with motherhood. Most of the time these influences lie beneath normal awareness and their influence is unconscious.

When people first become parents, their behavior sometimes becomes unusual for a while. For example a mother may become overconfident or excessively nervous. She may have a major loss of confidence followed by depression. She may even reject the baby. A mother may have unexplainable feelings of dread and persecution. If other people try to console her or give words of reassurance, the new mother may feel under attack. Simple tasks may become burdens yet she will not trust anyone else to do them for her. The mother may perceive the world around her to be a reflection of the chaos she feels inside. A dirty sink or an untidy room may be seen as symbols of failure.

Unconscious fantasies may be influencing her in negative ways. Much of her behavior may be influenced by an unconscious realization that her family doesn't need her. A mother may have secret fears about being inadequate and worry that she is unable to cope with a screaming baby. To accept help would be to admit failure.

A common parental fantasy played is that somewhere out there is the perfect mother or the perfect father. Social conditioning dictates that if there is an ideal, you are expected to live up to it. Often this is reinforced through the media and advertising. Apart from sex, nothing sells products better than the image of the perfect family with Supermom, Superdad, and two or three perfect kids. People are unconsciously urged to live up to impossible ideals by buying the product being promoted. When I worked in the advertising industry, I understood that one of the best subliminal sales messages was: "If you don't buy this, you will be a bad parent." Of course, the actual headline is never as blatant as that, but is cleverly disguised in subtle messages.

These unconscious fantasies about being the perfect parent can be used to manipulate or motivate people. They are very powerful forces. Nobody wants to fail as a parent, yet if the truth be known, new parents, at least initially, are badly equipped to deal with children. Yet the given fantasy is that mothers know what to do when a baby comes along. Unfortunately these idealizations and expectations may make it hard for some mothers (and fathers) to cope.

Many parents unconsciously play out the fantasy of being the perfect parent. A mother may try to keep up an unrealistic facade of being able to deal with anything and may make a big display to her friends and family that everything is under control. This pretence may mask her feelings of being unable to cope. She may not be able to live up to the collective fantasy of the ideal mother that society has created.

Followers of the Freudian psychoanalyst Melanie Klein claim that this perception of the mother as an all-powerful being becomes set in our consciousness during childhood. They believe that a little boy goes though an anxious period when he discovers that he has no womb and will never be able to be a mother himself. Because of this, the theory goes, many small boys are actively encouraged to despise girls and women and to deny any possibility that he has any desire to have a womb or breasts. He disguises his longing to be a mother by encouraging a girl to envy his having a penis. A girl has a crisis when she discovers she has no penis and at the same time cannot yet be a woman. In many instances these feelings of envy and despair result in denial of these powerful emotions in the girl. When she grows into a woman she may be unable to allow herself to have children since this would burst the dam of feelings she has been holding back.

Denial of infantile motherly feelings results in the image of the perfect parent becoming fixed in a child's mind. He or she will never succeed at becoming that parent. As a result of being cut off from the free flow of emotions, the fantasy becomes fossilized. For boys in particular, the idea of being a mother is rejected but his picture of motherhood does not develop as he grows up. Instead, from the age of two or three, he forms a fantasy of women based on his projected feelings of envy and jealousy.

## DREAMS AND FANTASIES ABOUT FATHERS

*"When I was a boy of fourteen, my father was so ignorant I could hardly stand to have the old man around. But when I got to be twenty-one, I was astonished at how much the old man had learned in seven years."*

MARK TWAIN

As with the mother image, dreams about your father may not be symbolic but may represent your father and your attitudes toward him. If your father (or mother, husband, wife, etc.) is dead, the dream may show how you are coming to terms with this bereavement. I have had many dream examples described to me where the sitter has been concerned that the spirit of their loved one is in some way distressed, because they have nightmares about the deceased person. The sleeper may dream of burying her father, but he keeps popping back up out of the ground like a zombie. This may actually show that the dreamer is unable to "bury her feelings" or may be refusing to face up to what has happened. At the time of a bereavement, and often many years later, a person may dream of being disowned by a dead parent, left in an orphanage, or abandoned in some way. These dreams express the lonely and painful feelings that come with bereavement. The dream may help resolve these difficult feelings.

A dream about your father dying may also

be a wish-fulfilling dream. Freud believed that children between the ages of four and seven go through a phase where they develop an incestuous desire for the parent of the opposite sex. The death of the father may symbolize the infantile desire to supplant him and possess the mother. Similarly it may show feelings of hostility that stem from childhood feelings of resentment or envy. In dreams the father is sometimes dethroned to enable the son to achieve a proper sense of his own value.

As an archetypal symbol the father represents the protector, the lawgiver, or ruler. He may appear in dreams as a king, emperor, wise old man, or as the sun, a weapon, or a phallus. Jung considered this important symbol to play a crucial psychological role in the destiny of the individual. Especially for men, the father archetype may be a symbol for an aspect of conscience. He may represent conventional moral opinions that may have been given to you by your own father.

In a woman's dream, the father may represent the one who generates affection. From a Freudian standpoint it may show the infantile desire of the daughter to supplant the mother and possess the father. This has been called the Electra complex. Although attributed to Freud, it is a term he never used. This is the female equivalent of the Oedipus complex. Some modern theorists maintain that the daughter's competition with her mother occurs during the preteen/teen years, with clashes over who is "sexy." Also, fathers must pull away from daughters at this age, which girls view as a withdrawal of affection.

# DREAMS AND FANTASIES ABOUT HUSBANDS AND WIVES

*"Sex alleviates tension. Love causes it."*

WOODY ALLEN

Dreams about your partner may simply be unconscious feelings about him or her. However you may also be projecting other feelings onto the dream figure. A husband may represent your father or the male side of your own personality. For a man, his wife appearing in a dream may represent his own female side or may be a symbol for his mother. The way a man relates to his wife, or a wife to her husband, may reflect their relationships with the parent of the opposite sex when they were children.

Carl Jung spoke about how lovers see their own personality reflected in the person they fall in love with. Jung called the personification of the feminine qualities in a man the anima, which emerges in dreams, the archetypal feminine symbolism within a man's unconscious. The animus is Jung's name for the personification of masculine psychological tendencies within a woman, the archetypal masculine symbolism within a woman's unconscious. According to Jung, the anima and animus draw their power from the collective unconscious, but they are also influenced by a person's individual experiences. In dreams the animus is more likely to be personified by multiple male figures, while the anima is frequently a single female.

People often fall in love with and marry a person that represents to them the anima or animus. In other words you tend to marry the "man or woman of your dreams."

I spoke earlier about how you might project your fantasies onto others and blame them for your faults. Similarly you might project everything good about yourself onto another persona and place the other person on a pedestal.

A man may project his anima onto the woman he courts. He may fantasize about her being the woman of his dreams and have an instant, powerful attraction for a woman he knows little about. This will be the case if a man identifies with the personal qualities within himself that are symbolically masculine. He may not recognize the importance of the symbolically feminine side of himself but rather will project these separated qualities within himself onto women. He will project his anima—those particular characteristics that are important components of his personal unconscious that carry a powerful emotional charge—onto a few women for whom he will then feel a strong and compelling emotion. Infatuation is one of the signs of anima projection, as is a compulsive possessiveness.

A man who has not integrated the anima qualities—such as emotion and intuition—into his psyche is apt to be taken over or "possessed" by these qualities at times. His emotional behavior may be acted out in childish and immature ways that are apparent to others but not to him.

A woman may do a similar thing when she falls in love with a man. A woman who identifies with those personal qualities that are symbolically feminine may not recognize qualities that are symbolically masculine as part of her own personality. These she projects onto men. In this case, she is projecting her animus. As in the man's case, she may suffer from compulsive attractions and possessiveness. This person has not consciously developed any of her symbolically masculine qualities such as logic, leadership, and need for independence. The result is that her personality is likely to be "possessed" by these qualities. She may appear opinionated, argumentative, or domineering to others, though she will not be aware of these traits within herself.

## DREAMS AND FANTASIES ABOUT BROTHERS AND SISTERS

*"Like branches on a tree we grow in different directions yet our roots remain as one. Each of our lives will always be a special part of the other."*

UNKNOWN

The anima and animus theme is often present in dreams about your brother or sister. A brother may represent the male side of a sister and vice versa. Jung claimed that childhood sibling rivalry and jealousy influence the dream symbols. For a male dreamer, a brother may represent the shadow side of the personality that is neglected and undeveloped. Sometimes this may include anti-social qualities that may be alarming to the dreamer. For a female dreamer the appearance of a sister in a dream may represent the shadow. And of course the dream may simply be about your relationship with your siblings.

# DREAMS AND FANTASIES ABOUT CHILDREN

*"The thing that impresses me most about North America is the way parents obey their children."*

EDWARD, DUKE OF WINDSOR

Dreams about babies and children may be simply an expression of your day-to-day concerns about your actual relationship with the children in the dream. It may also be an expression of your maternal instincts. As a symbol, a baby usually represents potential. A baby will express those aspects of yourself that have not fully developed. At first the dream may feature a pregnancy as a metaphor for new, inner qualities that are soon to emerge. A baby may represent something new in your life. It may also represent innocence, the aspect of you that remains pure and unsullied by contact with the world. If the baby cries, it may show that something arising from the unconscious is demanding your attention. Perhaps you feel upset about a new situation. Dead or grotesque babies may show inner fears that you need to address. A problem is beginning to emerge and you need to listen to your inner fears and act upon them.

Twins sometimes feature in dreams. Twins are often found in hero myths. The most well-known heroic twins are Romulus and Remus who were raised by a wolf and founded Rome. The same basic themes can be found in many other cultures. Navajo Indians tell the heroic story of the twin gods who are guided on their path to knowledge by the mysterious spider woman. In Navajo myths, the twins can also attain great power and become tyrannical—a theme illustrated by a story showing that an unbalanced self can disrupt the harmony of the psyche.

According to Jung, the twins represent opposite aspects of personality that need to be unified. Originally united in the mother's womb, they were forced apart at birth. However, they belong together and must be reunited. The twins demonstrate the two sides of a person's nature—the introvert, whose main attribute is the quality of reflection, and the extrovert, whose power can shape the world. When the difficult task of bringing the twins together is accomplished it shows how the personality has now attained a powerful symbiosis by becoming both reflective and active.

In dreams, a child may be a metaphor for the forgotten things in childhood. At the moment, your life is probably filled with all the usual problems associated with being an adult. When a child features in a dream it may be the unconscious reminding you about the innocent side of yourself. Perhaps it is saying that you would benefit by being more playful and taking a carefree attitude toward the issues that trouble you. As with the baby image, the symbol of the child can show possibilities. The dream may pave the way for future changes in personality. It may also represent the part of you that needs reassurance and security.

A recurrent theme in mythology is the "divine child." This mystical figure is often a hero or a savior. For example, in Greek mythology, Hercules strangled two threatening snakes, and in Christianity, baby Jesus became the redeemer who saves humanity from damnation. The divine child is the symbol of the true self, both vulnerable and possessed of great transforming power. In dreams it may show the growth of spirituality and self-knowledge and may reveal the omnipotent self that dwells within.

## DREAMS AND FANTASIES ABOUT GRANDPARENTS

*"If you live to the age of a hundred, you have it made because very, very few people die past the age of a hundred."*

GEORGE BURNS

Old age is associated with wisdom. Most children see their grandparents as more sympathetic figures than their parents. Parents must be obeyed, but a grandparent's advice is listened to and voluntarily applied. In dreams, grandparents therefore stand as symbols of wisdom that have stood the test of time. This wisdom may be the superior knowledge that arises from the unconscious.

A grandparent may also appear in a dream as a guiding figure. Wise figures often appear in dreams if you have a spiritual drive toward self-knowledge. As well as a grandfather figure, the wise old man may take various forms such as a king, wizard, prophet, teacher, guru, or priest. Similarly the wise old woman may appear as a goddess, earth mother, prophet, teacher, or saint.

Jung called these figures "*mana* personalities" (from the Melanesian word for "holiness" or "the divine"). These are symbols for the power and wisdom that lies in the deepest parts of the psyche. Jung called them mana personalities because in primitive communities anyone having extraordinary powers or wisdom was thought to be filled with mana (holiness). The quality of these figures can be awesome and sometimes frightening, though in the form of a grandparent it is likely to be more benign. Dreams that contain mana figures are extremely important and represent a time of great spiritual progress and opportunity. A whole new dimension to your awareness is opening for you.

## THE SPIRITUAL FAMILY

*"All happy families are alike; each unhappy family is unhappy in its own way."*

LEO TOLSTOY,
OPENING LINE OF *ANNA KARENINA*

It is clear that your parental and family influences play an important part in shaping you. A happy childhood is clearly a benefit that helps you learn to cope with the world. Many theories of psychology consider childhood influences among the most important factors in making you who you are now. However, a bad childhood does not necessarily mean you are going to be wracked by neurosis. I have met a number of exemplary people who were orphans. History has shown that childhood experiences have not stopped many individuals from shining despite their privations. Edgar Allen Poe started his life in an orphanage, as did Dave Thomas, the owner and founder of the Wendy's Restaurant chain. And, of course, Moses was an orphan.

Similarly, many people do not flower until later in life and may be slow early developers. Albert Einstein did not begin to speak until he was three years old, and according to some accounts, five, or even seven years old. He didn't learn to tie his own shoelaces until he was thirteen. Clearly, although childhood is one of the most important periods in life, countless examples show that it is not the only factor that determines future potential.

The best way to test the above would be to design an experiment in which someone is given a terrible first three years of life after which everything becomes okay. If early-childhood experiences determine the future, those first three years should have a lasting impression. No matter how right things are later on, the person would not be able to recover. However, people who have a terrible childhood do not automatically turn into psychopaths or twisted individuals. Usually the single most important factor that determines the success of a person is who the person marries.

Clearly, many other environmental influences shape a person's life. A potentially successful person may be thwarted by an illness or a tragic event that prevents the person from moving forward. But perhaps there is another factor that scientists have not yet considered. I suggested earlier that childhood games may be influenced by conditions brought forward from past lives. Could it be that family bonds are also determined by factors that existed before the time of birth?

In the Western world, people are seen as individuals with their own souls. However, some spiritual traditions believe that this apparent separation of the individual is a temporary state. They claim that there is a group soul or oversoul, and individuals are part of that larger soul. Fragments of this greater spirit incarnate into this world for experiences that will contribute to the oversoul when they return to it. Only an infinitesimal part of the whole individuality manifests in physical form on Earth. You do not lose your earthly individuality when you eventually merge with the group soul, for it is like a stream that flows into a river.

According to this theory, your family and those you care about most in life are part of your own self, for you share the same group soul. Dreams about the family would therefore not be symbols but real parts of your being.

I do not subscribe to this idea per se, but understand there to be a group soul that is a linking of individuals who have shared many past lives together and hold common karma. These are your soul mates. Some people call it the Soul Clan or Soul Family. From this soul group arise many—but not all—of the major relationships in your life such as parents, children, business partners, best friends, and so on. Someone you consider your arch-enemy is also likely to be within your greater soul group. These are relationships based upon learning and development through interaction with people who are not always in harmony with our own ideas. There is nothing more challenging to the soul than an ex-partner who may be keen to kick your spiritual complacency into a higher gear.

The way you fantasize about your parents as a child and your reactions to them as an adult may, therefore, have nothing to do with infantile sexuality or a good or bad childhood, and so on. Your relationship may be based on direct experiences brought forward from former lives. Many believe that people in a group soul tend to incarnate together. Those with a very close bond will often be born into the same family. The result could be that your mother from a past life could be your daughter or son in this one. The same may happen with members of the group soul with whom you share a difficult karma. For example, an ex-husband from a former life may be your father in this one.

Clearly the potential permutations for past, present, and future relationships within the group soul are great indeed. It is important to sort out your relationships, as they will follow you into the afterlife and into future lives. Perhaps Freud really did have a "devouring mother" in a past life! Maybe you shared an unfortunate karmic bond with one of your own parents which has brought difficulties.

The human condition is a complex one that I believe cannot yet be explained by the rules of psychology. There are many factors at work that mold you into becoming who you are. Clearly you may sometimes have hidden fantasies that motivate you below the surface of your awareness, some of which originate in childhood but some of which may originate in previous lives. Dreams and fantasies may give insight into what these past lives may have been and what hidden forces now influence behavior.

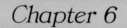

# Chapter 6

# SPIRIT AND SOUL

*"Everything of which I know but of which I cannot at the moment think; everything of which I was once conscious but have now forgotten; everything perceived by my senses but not noted by my conscious mind; everything which involuntarily and without paying attention to it, I feel, think, remember, want, and do; all future things that are taking shape in me and will some time come to consciousness. All this is the content of the unconscious."*

CARL JUNG,
THE WISDOM OF THE DREAM VIDEO SERIES, A MAN OF DREAMS.

Dreams are a doorway to the hidden part of you. They reveal the fantasies about who you think you are and who you would like to be. They expose your most secret fantasies about sex, power, money, career, and family. Dreams also highlight the anxieties and fears you have about your situation now and problems that you have brought forward from your distant past. Using the language of metaphor, allegory, and symbolism, dreams may give tremendous insight into yourself and the problems you face in day-to-day life. They highlight your clandestine fantasies and fears and

provide you with solutions to help make your life better.

But there is another function of dreams well beyond the emotions, mind, and conditions of everyday life. Dreams can put you in touch with the soul. Dreams help address the big questions about the meaning and purpose of life. Hero myths deal with these issues as well, as do images of heroes that appear in dreams, the mystical journey to higher consciousness, and the quest for wholeness of the psyche. Understanding how dreams can connect you to the ancient, forgotten part of yourself can give direct spiritual insight.

Many people today have completely lost touch with the spiritual side of their nature. Western society has an unprecedented level of prosperity, yet a great many people are deeply unhappy. The cure for this malady of the soul comes by reconnecting to the unconscious, by having direct intuition of the meaning and purpose of your life. Your dreams and fantasies may already hint at how to find the pathway that leads to this insight. Perhaps the imagery you use in your everyday language or your artistic tastes speak of fantasies that are prompting you to embark on the great spiritual exploration of yourself. For example, Celtic art and symbolism are popular fashion accessories at the time of writing. Have you ever considered why these themes attract people? Could it be that a large proportion of the population hopes somehow to escape from the air-conditioned security of modern society and get back in touch with the pagan part of themselves? The soul yearns to again tell heroic tales around a sparking fire at night, dance pagan dances, or howl with wolves. Similarly, the current fashion for Native American, Far Eastern, and pagan symbolism shows that many people today are looking back to rediscover their collective spiritual roots. This cross-cultural ancestry is still alive and appears again in modern society. It is part of our collective unconscious.

The collective unconscious is that part of a person that is the storehouse for the collective, inherited contents, the instincts and the archetypes. It is the reservoir of the experience of the species, a sort of knowledge a people are all born with. One of Jung's favorite metaphors was that it is like the ocean that has its calms and storms, monsters and mermaids, and which can be a force of either creativity or destruction. From the collective unconscious springs the power of creativity, which can be placed in the service of the individual.

But where does the collective unconscious get this information archive from? How can a collective memory be passed from one generation to another? Natural selection ensures that the best behavior patterns are inherited, but I cannot conceive of a way that it could pass on racial memories in the form of symbolism and archetypes. The given wisdom is that genes mutate, and those that are useful survive and are handed down. But there is nothing to suggest that they can be altered by mental means.

The collective unconscious Jung describes appears to be more than an accumulation of hidden mental processes. It has a life of its own and is like a database for the wisdom of the ages. Rather than existing inside your head, it appears to exist "out there." I have no doubt that telepathy is real and that minds can connect without the use of the known senses. Mind-to-mind communication would account for the cases where people share exactly the same dream. But could it be that the mind can link to a greater collective consciousness similar to the way computers are linked together via the Internet?

Suppose you could link your consciousness to the collective knowledge of all time? You would know the ancient past and perhaps the future too. I believe that this is what Jung really discovered when he formulated the theory of the archetypes and the collective unconscious. He stumbled upon a portal to

DANCING AS AN EXPRESSION OF THE SOUL

this fragment of interconnected consciousness. Jung observed that these feelings of connectedness that occur when the inner and outer world synchronize, leave an indelible impression on those who experience them. "I felt as though Grace had once again nudged the details of my life in such a way as to show me with a certainty beyond proof that I was and am not an isolated individual, but an integral part of the far vaster 'web' of all that is—a web which I find consistently more 'intelligent' and 'gracious' than I am."

## DEATH AND OTHER WORLDS

*"It would be a great satisfaction to me if I could convince myself and others on unimpeachable evidence of the existence of telepathic processes."*

SIGMUND FREUD

If someone were to say to you that you are a "dreamer," you would probably be offended, as it implies that you live a life of fantasy and have an unrealistic attitude to your circumstances. But dreamers were once the pioneers of human civilization. From ancient times, people understood that dreams could bring answers to perplexing questions. More importantly, they believed that dreams came from a divine source. God speaks to his prophets through dreams—people who have shaped the course of human history more than any banker, warlord, or ruler. Most of the great religions of the world have been built upon the foundations of dreams, meditation, and introspection. These techniques take you on an inner journey that connects you to the memory of the cosmos. Who knows what the great dreamers and seers of old discovered from their spiritual journeys through this interconnected world of mind? Perhaps the sleeping shamans traveled to other webs of awareness where they met beings from other dimensions or galaxies that they later described in mythology.

## Talking with the Dead

In my archives I have many instances of people who claim they have spoken to a dead loved one in a dream. Skeptics may dismiss this as fantasy, but there is often empirical proof to show that a real spirit communication has taken place. Information may be revealed that the dreamer could not possibly know about otherwise. For example, a dreamer has met a dead parent in a dream and been shown where to find the missing will. Or the dreamer has been given details by the dead person that initially appeared to be nonsense but proved to be accurate when checked by a third party.

I am certain that the dead can communicate with the living through dreams. For example, soon after my maternal grandmother died, my father awoke from a dream and saw her standing at the foot of the bed. Seeing her shook him, but he was also puzzled because she was wearing a radiant pink color. Later that day my aunt returned from the mortuary and said. "I have just been to see Nan. She looks wonderful. They have made her look beautiful and she is wearing a very bright pink shroud." My father had always assumed that shrouds were white.

Perhaps my grandmother didn't like the color! Although much of the proof of spirit communication in these instances is anecdotal,

DO DREAMS TRANSCEND DEATH?

there is a great deal to suggest that real communication has taken place. The accumulated weight of evidence collected by paranormal researchers is overwhelmingly in favor of the premise that the dead can speak to the living in dreams. I believe that dreams such as these are often—but not always—direct communication with the next stage of life through this fragment of consciousness. Jung's experiences support this, and in his writings he has conceded that sometimes it is possible for the dead to speak to the living in dreams.

## Death Premonitions

Dreams may sometimes predict a death. Just before my sister got married, my paternal grandmother had a dream that my sister turned up for the ceremony wearing a black wedding dress. My grandmother was terribly upset by the dream and confided in my aunt.

Soon after the wedding, the groom was diagnosed with cancer. Within a year he was dead. Clearly in this case the dream was not a fantasy but predicted a specific event. Nonetheless it has to be said that most dreams about death are an expression of the emotional condition of the dreamer rather than predictions about the future. They may represent the ending of one phase so that another may begin. For example, a death dream may occur after a divorce, job change, or an examination. Dreams of death suggest that something is about to end so that something fresh and new can begin.

Dreams about death are usually symbolic and in most instances are unlikely to forecast an actual event. If the dead person you dream about is someone you know, this may represent a part of yourself that has been neglected.

For example, to dream of your mother dying could represent the death of the motherly side of your nature. You may need to learn to be more caring and maternal, or perhaps plans that you have nurtured have been killed off?

Dreams about death can also reveal your feelings about people. You may "wish someone was dead" perhaps not literally, but symbolically you wish the person no longer had an influence on your life. Similarly, a corpse may represent an issue that you wish were "dead and buried." You may feel emotionally spent and may need to shrug off old prejudices that are preventing you from realizing your growth. The dead body may also represent aspects of yourself that you do not want to accept. You may feel that it is a symbol to show how you are buried in feelings that are overwhelming you. It may express extreme tiredness such as being "dead beat."

If there is a feeling of hope in your dream, then your dream may be showing you that a change is imminent and a positive transformation is possible. If you feel fear, it may show that the death represents something you are avoiding consciously or unconsciously. If you dream of dying, it probably shows that you are emotionally at your lowest ebb and feel disconnected and helpless.

Freud believed that there are two primary forces in the human psyche: *Eros* (the life instinct), which covers all the self-preserving and erotic instincts, and *Thanatos* (the death instinct), which covers all the instincts toward aggression, self-destruction, and cruelty. According to his theory, *Thanatos* is the irrational urge to destroy the source of all sexual energy in the annihilation of the self. Freud placed sexual drives at the center of human life and proposed that sexual energy (*libido*) is the single most important motivating force in adult life. This drive includes the drive for any kind of bodily pleasure. *Thanatos* is the opposite—the force that denies pleasure and seeks death. From a Freudian point of view, dreams and fantasies about death represent a denial of the sexual drive.

Eventually death will come to everyone, yet few people are prepared to contemplate their own mortality. In dreams people may ask the avoided question: "What will happen to me when I die?" This issue becomes particularly important to the terminally ill.

Some fascinating studies have been made of the dreams of the dying. In particular, the work of Marie-Louise von Franz explored the dreams of patients prior to sudden or anticipated death. One would expect the dreams to be concerned with the immanent termination of life, but their common denominator does not seem to be simply an end to earthly life but a transformation in preparation for the afterlife. It is as if the unconscious mind knows something the conscious mind doesn't. It anticipates that death is not the end.

Research indicates that the dreams of people facing death are a preparation for a profound inner transformation. The symbolism and imagery anticipate a continuation of the life process. Often these symbols correspond to the teachings of various religions yet may also employ many mythical images. These dreams help the individual accept the upcoming event and remove the terrible uncertainty that many feel about death.

If you were terminally ill, you would be less inclined to turn away from the concept of death. In dreams you may have the possibility of addressing this great fear. You need not wait until your time has come to die. Instead, your dreams will open the doorway to your higher awareness that knows the truth behind the illusion of life. Part of you has direct awareness of the other world that lies beyond this life, and you can access this information via your dreams.

## THE PROCESS OF BECOMING

*"The experience of the alchemists was, in a sense, my experience, and their world was my world....I had stumbled upon the historical counterpart of my psychology of the unconscious. The possibility of a comparison with alchemy, and the uninterrupted intellectual chain back to Gnosticism, gave substance to my psychology."*

CARL JUNG

Techniques such as meditation, positive thinking, and self-discipline encourage better spiritual values but also are methods of bringing direct realization of spiritual truth. Dreams mirror these conscious spiritual decisions to progress, and they reflect this using symbolism. Furthermore, the cause of much unhappiness comes from inner poverty, which may prompt the dreamer to embark upon the inner, spiritual journey.

Self-realization is not only a rational process but one that requires complete inner transformation. This process demands the sacrifice of all that is base in the human condition in favor of the higher ideals of the spirit. Spiritual wholeness is attained by inner transformation, purification, and the integration of the neglected parts of the psyche.

Jung realized that this process of becoming had its counterpart in medieval alchemy. Alchemy was a medieval precursor to modern chemistry, which believed that it could produce gold from base metals. The premise of alchemy is mistaken, as elements cannot be altered by chemical means. However, Jung was interested in the mystical branch of alchemy and he undertook a painstaking study of its vast literature. In 1952, Jung wrote *Psychology and Alchemy*, in which he proposed that the alchemists were dealing primarily with "psychic processes [of individuation/growth] expressed in pseudo-chemical language." Jung proposed that alchemy was not a precursor of chemistry but a challenge to theology. According to Jung, alchemists did not seek to turn base metal into gold but to bring about their own inner transformation.

Although as a religion alchemy has all but ceased to be, as a mystical system it can still offer spiritual guidance. As it is not institutionalized, it retains an intimate, non-prescriptive relationship with the collective unconscious. It addresses similar problems to ones faced now but from a different historical perspective. The true goal of alchemy is to transform the dull, everyday lead of normal awareness into "golden" consciousness and higher awareness. In this state of being, you attain the world of spirit through modes of perception that are usually beyond reach.

Jung noticed in the alchemical treaties similar obscure symbols to those found in the dreams of patients who had never seen an alchemical text. These dreams included images such as a dragon swallowing the sun or eating its own tail, figures that are half-man/half-woman, golden trees, mandalas, twin fountains, and mystical marriages of medieval kings and queens. Jung concluded that the strange images of his patients' dreams came from deep levels of the collective unconscious.

The fantasies of the alchemists depicted strange symbols that represented the totality of spiritual wisdom, knowingly or unknowingly accessed from the collective unconscious. In their attempt to transmute base metals into gold, the alchemists were in fact trying to change themselves. Jung argued that the alchemists were attempting to transform and heal their personalities, which were divided and full of inner conflicts, to bring them into a state of harmony and wholeness. The chemical processes represented the dissolving of all the parts of their old personality into a single unified personality expressed in the alchemical maxim "*solve et coagula*," dissolve and solidify.

Just as astrology was the precursor for astronomy, so alchemy gave birth to modern chemistry. However, alchemy was also an investigation of the psyche and a direct way to experience the unconscious.

A QUEEN SIGNIFIES A CHANGE OF CONSCIOUSNESS

# WITHIN AND WITHOUT

*"When I pray, coincidences happen; when I don't, they don't."*

ARCHBISHOP WILLIAM TEMPLE

One of the precepts that the alchemists followed was the "doctrine of correspondences." This is a mystical belief that links together seemingly dissimilar forces and material substances and claims that all things are joined by an unbreakable bond. The eighteenth-century mystic and scientist Emanuel Swedenborg said that everything that occurs in the visible world also appears in the invisible world. If you can imagine that all things in the world are some form of vibration, then it follows that certain correlations or correspondences might exist in other groups.

In addition to the doctrine or correspondences, the alchemists proposed that every person is also a miniature reflection of the whole universe. The alchemists called this the microcosm, a "little cosmos" that is a model of the macrocosm, "the great cosmos." The concept can be summarized by the words that are inscribed on the alchemical tablet called *The Emerald Tablet*, by Hermes Trismegistus, which in cryptic wording says: "as above, so below." The significance of this phrase is that it is believed to hold the key to all mysteries. This maxim supposes that man is the counterpart of God on Earth and that God is man's counterpart in heaven. It is a statement of an ancient belief that man's actions on Earth parallel the actions of God in heaven

According to this ancient theory, it is therefore possible for the mind to influence the events in the world. This is certainly the belief of magicians who hold that influences are made by an imaginative act accompanied by the will that the desired change occur. The magician knows with certainty that for magical changes to occur, he must will them to happen and firmly believe they will happen.

It may be that dreams and fantasies have the same power to affect the world. Jung noticed that meaningful coincidences often occur around important psychological events. Jung called this acausal connecting principle "synchronicity," a term to describe the occurrence of meaningful coincidence. This would include inner psychic happenings such as dreams, visions, and premonitions that are accompanied by a corresponding outer physical event that could not have been causally connected. Some psychologists claim that most cases of extrasensory perception are examples of synchronicity.

One of Jung's first experiences of synchronicity happened in 1909, while he was meeting with Freud. They had been discussing psychic phenomena, and Freud had expressed skepticism at the genuineness of the phenomena. As he spoke, both of them heard an explosive noise. Freud hesitated, then continued the conversation, only to be interrupted again by another loud bang that clearly came from somewhere in the room in which they were talking.

Freud looked a little shaken but attributed the sound to the contraction of pipes in the heating system. Jung, however, considered it to have another cause and referred to the noises as "catalytic exteriorization phenomena," which in simple terms means that Jung was somehow creating the effect by producing a meaningful coincidence.

Another strange instance happened after Jung had a vision of a fantasy guide he named Philemon. Jung painted the figure into his spiritual diary, which he called "The Red Book." His discovery of the sage was a turning point and inspired him to formulate his theory of the collective unconscious. Philemon's presence revealed to Jung "the crucial insight that there are things in the psyche which I do not produce, but which produce themselves and have their own life."

Philemon had a long white beard, a halo, and wore the wings of a kingfisher. Some hours later while walking in his garden by the lake, Jung stumbled upon a dead kingfisher. The bird was very rare, and Jung had never seen one there before, nor was he to see one again. In many cultures, the kingfisher is a symbol of inspiration. For Jung, this was a striking example of a meaningful coincidence and inspired him to formulate and qualify his theory of synchronicity.

Jung quotes a number of instances when startling meaningful coincidences took place near him. For example, the doorbell would often ring when Jung was feeling "something is about to happen."

A particularly intriguing incident is quoted in Jung's book *The Structure and Dynamics of the Psyche*. A young female patient was proving hard to work with because she had the attitude that she always knew better. Her extensive education gave her an overrational view of the world. Jung needed something to happen that would help crack this wall of rationality. Jung wrote:

"Well, I was sitting opposite her one day, with my back to the window, listening to her flow of rhetoric. She had an impressive dream the night before, in which someone had given her a golden scarab (a beetle—in this case carved into jewelry), a costly piece of jewelry. While she was still telling me this dream, I heard something behind me gently tapping on the window. I turned round and saw that it was a fairly large insect that was knocking against the windowpane from outside in the obvious effort to get into the dark room. This seemed to me very strange. I opened the window immediately and caught the insect in the air as it flew in. It was a scarabaeid beetle, or common rose-chafer, whose gold-green color most nearly resembles that of a golden scarab. I handed the beetle to my patient with the words, 'here is your scarab.' This experience punctured the desired hole in her rationalism and broke the ice of her intellectual resistance. The treatment could now continue with satisfactory results."

The propitious timing of events indicated that the transcendental meaning of both the scarab in the dream and the insect in the room was that the patient needed to be liberated from her excessive rationalism.

In 1944, at the age of 68 Jung had a severe heart attack. While hovering between life and death, he experienced curious visions, in one of which he was hovering out of his body and above the earth. Ahead of him he saw a Hindu temple built inside a meteor. Here he met his doctor, who was dressed in the ancient garb of a priest of Kos. Jung was convinced that if he recovered, his doctor would have to die in his place. In fact the doctor did die, just as Jung started to recover.

Jung had many other visions during his period of illness. He understood that he had a second chance at life and no longer cared what his fellow scientists thought about his mystical ideas. Jung decided that he would no longer make a secret of his lifelong interest in the occult. In 1949 he wrote about the "acausal connecting principle" called synchronicity. In the following year he wrote the paper, "On Synchronicity," which was later expanded into a book.

## PSYCHIC DREAMS

*"There are few persons, even among the calmest thinkers, who have not occasionally been startled into a vague yet thrilling half-credence in the supernatural, by coincidences of so seemingly marvelous a character that, as mere coincidences, the intellect has been unable to receive them."*

EDGAR ALLEN POE

Since ancient times, people have believed it is possible to predict the future with dreams. The Temple of Apollo in Delphi, for example, housed the most important oracle of ancient Greece, known as Pythia. Only the wealthy could afford the fees of the oracle, and many questions of state were decided by what the Delphic oracle foretold. The ancient Greeks built more than three hundred temples and shrines that were used as places where a person could sleep and receive messages from the gods while sleeping. They believed that as they slept, the gods would answer questions or foretell the future with a dream. In particular, the sleeper would be visited by Hypnos, the god of sleep, who would fan him with the wings of his headdress.

Similarly, the ancient Egyptians believed that dreams could foresee the future. They also believed that certain places were conducive to dreaming. An Egyptian text attributed to King Merikare, the pharaoh who ruled from about 2070 B.C.E., tells of the ruler's dreams and what they might foretell. Dream divination (oneiromancy) can also be found in both Old and New Testaments of the Bible. The Bible contains accounts of people whose dreams foretold the future and who influenced decisions of kings or pharaohs.

But is it really possible to see into time? You may have had a tantalizing glimpse of the future yourself. Many ordinary people who make no claim to having special powers have written to me to say that they've seen the future. "I awoke from a bad dream at exactly 9:03. In the dream I saw my father collapse outside the local hospital," says Pamela K. "Exactly two months later, at 9:03 A.M., my father collapsed and died at the exact spot that I had dreamt about."

Many people have contacted me to say that their terrible, unwanted visions of the future can be very worrying. "I kept having terrible repetitive nightmares of a nuclear disaster by a tall tower," says Mrs. F. "I would thrash in my sleep and was heard to call out, 'The Russians! The Russians!' The meaning of my nightmares was revealed on the television some weeks later. I saw on the news a picture of the very tower that I had just been dreaming about: the Chernobyl power station in Russia."

I get hundreds of e-mails and letters that would indicate that many people have prophetic dreams. It is likely that everyone has psychic powers that lie dormant in the mind waiting to be triggered. Scientists call these powers Extra Sensory Perception (ESP) and subdivide them into telepathy (communicating by thought), clairvoyance (seeing events without using the five senses), psychokinesis (influencing matter by thought, e.g., spoon bending) and precognition (seeing the future). Scientists have studied these psychic powers since the 1930s, when Professor J. B. Rhine, at Duke University, in the U.S.A., made a systematic study in the laboratory. He used as his evidence card-guessing games and discovered that many students, who had been randomly selected from the university campus, could predict which cards would come next in a randomly shuffled pack of Zener cards. Their scores were far above what would be expected from chance alone.

The research into ESP continues to this day. Experiments in precognition, which started in the ancient Greek temple of Apollo, were, ironically enough, secretly carried out on the Apollo 14 space mission in the 1960s, by astronaut Edgar D. Mitchell.

In the 1960s, Dr. Montague Ullman conducted some of the first experiments into dream-ESP at the Maimonides Medical Center in New York. His team discovered that when people dream, their eye muscles move very rapidly under closed eyelids. They found that this rapid eye movement (REM) happened during dreams and that this was the best time to conduct experiments in dream telepathy. When the subjects began showing REM, senders tried to use telepathy to transmit images to them. When the REM burst ended, the sleeper was awakened and asked about the dreams and the dream images. In many instances, the dreams contained the same images as the picture telepathically projected during the experiment.

In a second series of tests carried out over eight nights, it was concluded that the dream report successfully linked with the picture on six occasions. This was a 75 percent success rate. Chance alone would have produced only one correct link between the picture being transmitted and the dream over eight consecutive nights. "Perhaps our most basic finding," wrote Ullman, "is the scientific demonstration of Freud's statement: 'Sleep creates favorable conditions for telepathy.'"

## Déjà Vu

Have you ever experienced the eerie feeling that occurs when you're halfway through a conversation and suddenly everything that's being said seems strangely familiar? It's like watching a movie and partway through realizing you've already seen it. Except this is real life. You've lived this incident once before. Sometimes the same feeling comes out of the blue in the most mundane situations. You feel that you've lived this episode before.

This experience, called "déjà vu," translates from the French as "seen before." Usually it lasts only a few seconds but there are pathological cases on record where the subject has prolonged or even a constant feeling of déjà vu. The phenomenon is experienced occasionally by the majority of normal people usually under conditions of fatigue or heightened sensitivity.

Science still can't adequately explain it. One neurological theory says that déjà vu is caused when the two hemispheres of the brain temporarily lose their synchronicity. This results in the strange feeling of familiarity as one side of the brain receives input a fraction of a second after the other. Many psychologists say that déjà vu is a form of paramnesia, where experience reminds you of repressed memories you'd prefer not to recall. It may be simply that the experience reminds you of real, partly recalled events or perhaps, as some claim, déjà vu may be the recall of a prophetic dream.

EXPERIMENT

### HERE'S A FUN EXPERIMENT TO TRY:

Some dreams are so vivid, they are closer to visions than dreams. These often reveal remarkable predictions about the future. You are not captive to the present. In dreams you become a master of time and can have clairvoyant glimpses of what may come.

In 1927, J. W. Dunne proposed that during sleep people enter a different dimension of time in which past, present, and future become intertwined. The insights received during this state of consciousness are perceived through the subconscious, which translates insights into symbolic form. Often a vision of a future event is distorted or turned into an allegory. Be careful, therefore,

to distinguish between what is fact and what is a distortion or symbolic representation of your own anxieties.

There's a state between sleeping and waking that psychologists call hypnagogic dreaming. It can happen just before you fall asleep, and if you've already experienced this you'll know how remarkable it is. These "dreams" are a flow of brilliant vivid images which, if you can maintain the state, can be manipulated. Hypnagogic dreams contain potent omens of the future.

To test their prophetic power, it's a good idea to set a target subject to dream about. It's better to choose something you're not emotionally involved with. So for this experiment, try to predict "tomorrow's news today."

**Step 1**: Put a pencil and paper by the side of your bed so you can write down your insights.

**Step 2:** Now you must choose a target subject to dream about. For this experiment you are going to try to gain insight about the future of a well-known celebrity. So get yourself a copy of a people-orientated newspaper or magazine and decide whom you would like to know more about. It is best that it be someone you find interesting. Cut out a photo of the person while you're in bed. This will reinforce your messages to the subconscious.

**Step 3:** Look at the photo as you lie in bed and prepare to go to sleep. Be aware of your conscious thoughts about what you think

VIVID IMAGES OCCUR JUST BEFORE SLEEP

will happen to this person in the near future. Now write their name down on the notepad together with this message to your subconscious: "Tell me this person's future."

**Step 4:** As you drift into sleep, try to remain in a state of awareness between wakefulness and sleep. Hold your attention in this state as long as you can. Let yourself think in pictures rather than words. With a little effort you will see a brilliant stream of imagery in your mind's eye. Focus on these images and retain them.

**Step 5:** Now visualize a page from a newspaper or magazine. There's no heading yet. It's a blank page. Fantasize again about your chosen celebrity. What photograph appears on the page? Does anything about the photo give you clues to upcoming events?

**Step 6:** Perhaps a headline appears, and perhaps you can intuitively hear the words of an imaginary newscaster. Now pull yourself back from the brink of sleep and write down your impressions. If nothing comes to you, don't worry; just let yourself go and write down your dream in the morning. As soon as you wake up, write it down, even if it isn't about the person. You may find an accurate prediction is woven into the plot of the dream. Some of the things in the dream may not make sense until events unfold.

**Step 7:** You can try the same experiment over a series of nights with different celebrities. Pay careful attention to your notes. You may dis-

cover that you know the gossip way ahead of the Hollywood columnists!

## FANTASY AND COINCIDENCE

*"Chains of more-than-coincidence occur so often in my life that, if I am forbidden to call them supernatural hauntings, let me call them a habit. Not that I like the word 'supernatural'; I find these happenings natural enough, though superlatively unscientific."*

ROBERT GRAVES, *THE WHITE GODDESS*

Could it be that the dream mode is one with the opportunity for inner and outer events to come together? Synchronicity is not merely coincidence, but coincidence that specifically bridges the "subjective" and "objective," "inner" and "outer" worlds. It is my belief that certain dreams go beyond fantasy and put people in touch with other levels of reality. If you tap this source, you can change the reality of your normal, everyday life. Strange things start to happen.

My work as a medium brings me in contact with many people who have embarked on a spiritual search. Often people explain to me that they have been led to have a consultation with me by a series of strange coincidences. Most of these are not remarkable. For example, they may read about me in a newspaper, then pick up one of my books, then someone recommends me, and then they stumble across my website—all in the course of a few hours. This type of coincidence is more likely now that I am well-known, but it used to happen when I ran a design business and kept my work as a medium secret.

Strange coincidences are banal and appear to have no spiritual meaning. However, it may be that when you think a lot about coincidences, they start to happen. For example, moments after writing the paragraph above, I had an extraordinary telephone call from a BBC producer requesting my appearance on a program about "strange coincidences"! They were not as surprised as you might think when I told them I had been writing about coincidences just moments before they called. Equally odd coincidences had happened to many of the other contributors they contacted, many of whom were skeptics or cynical scientists.

There are many arguments against coincidence. For example, statistics show that in a room of 23 people it is pretty certain that two will share the same birthday. What may appear to be a coincidence is in fact statistically probable. A skeptic may point out many seemingly impossible situations that are in fact more likely to happen than you would expect. I once mentioned to a friend that magpies are considered unlucky, and that superstition claims that in order to ward off the bad luck, they should be saluted. The next time I met my friend, he said, "I wish you hadn't told me about the magpies. Now I see them everywhere and I am endlessly saluting! People are beginning to think I'm crazy." Magpies are a common bird in the United Kingdom, but until I mentioned the unlucky superstition, my friend had never noticed them. Many people tend to notice apparent coincidences when they look for them. Traditional omens and auguries are based on this.

But this does not explain the strange way coincidences appear to "attach" themselves to some people. Here is an example of an odd coincidence in my family, dating back to 1884.

Richard Parker, my grandfather's seventeen-year-old cousin, was employed as a cabin boy on the *Mignonette* when it set sail for Australia from my home town of Southampton, in the United Kingdom. They were 1,600 miles from land when the South Atlantic hurricane broke. The *Mignonette* was hit by huge waves and sank. In the panic to board the lifeboats, the crew was unable to salvage any provisions or water except two small tins of turnips.

The crew had very little to eat or drink for 19 days and became desperate. Richard Parker drank sea water and became delirious. Captain Dudley considered drawing lots to choose a victim to feed the remaining crew. Brooks was against any killing whatsoever, Stephens was indecisive, so the captain decided to kill Parker as he was near death and had no dependents.

The resulting court case fascinated Victorian society and became the best documented study of cannibalism in the United Kingdom. Dudley, Stephens, and Brooks were each sentenced to six months hard labor and later emigrated.

But the story has a strange twist. Half a century before the grisly events, in 1837, Edgar Allan Poe wrote *The Narrative of Arthur Gordon Pym of Nantucket*. This book tells of four shipwrecked men who, after many days' privation, drew lots to decide who should be killed and eaten.

The cabin boy drew the short straw. His name was Richard Parker!

My Uncle Keith, thought that Richard's story would make an interesting theme for a radio play and began to plan a synopsis. At that time, to supplement his writer's income, he reviewed books. The first book to arrive for review was *The Sinking of the Mignonette*. A few weeks later he was asked to review a play, among a collection of short plays, called *The Raft*. It was a comedy for children. There was nothing sinister about it at all, apart from the cover illustration. Three men seemed to threaten a young boy, which was completely out of keeping with the play's tone. *The Raft* was written by someone named Richard Parker.

In the summer of 1993, my parents took in three Spanish language students. My father told them about Richard Parker one evening over supper (probably in an attempt to keep the food bills down). The television was on in the background. All conversation stopped when a local program started talking about the remarkable story. Dad went on to break the silence by saying that weird coincidences always occurred whenever Richard's tale was mentioned. He then told them about Edgar Allan Poe.

Two of the girls went white. "Look what I bought today," one said. She reached into her bag and pulled out a copy of the Poe story. "So have I!" said the other girl. Both had gone shopping that day and independently bought the very same book containing the Richard Parker story. And, as if events are trying to make my story totally unbelievable, my father told the same story to his language students the following year. Again one of the girls pulled a copy of the Poe book out of her bag!

Recently I received a letter from a man who had read another article I wrote about Richard Parker. Immediately after he'd read it he gave professional advice to a friend, who was complaining about his employer. His employer had been researching his family tree and said to the person who wrote to me: "Well, I reckon this riding roughshod over legal procedures is in his blood. This guy is into tracing his ancestors, and one of them was a sea captain named Dudley who was done for eating a cabin boy and cheated at drawing lots...."

The Richard Parker story shows that sometimes the normal structure of time has flaws in it. Perhaps Poe saw into the future and wrote about events that were to take place 50 years later. Perhaps the public attention the case was given around the world created a sort of mental energy that continues to try to express itself whenever a person contemplates what happened. I am not inclined to think it is Richard Parker's ghost. I have had reliable evidence and a drawing given by the famous medium Coral Polge—who knew nothing of the story. Everything suggests that Richard's spirit is at peace.

I believe that weird coincidences like this demonstrate that sometimes there is a twist in the fabric of time, like a missing frame in a movie that causes the screen to flicker momentarily. The arrow of time has somehow gone astray and there are occasional flaws in reality as most people understand it. Coincidences, however banal, may make people ponder the nature of space and time. They demonstrate that reality may not be quite as it is ordinarily believed to be.

Many incidences of coincidence cannot be dismissed as statistical anomalies. Some of the latest theories and observations of particle physics and cosmology suggest that at the extremes of the universe reality behaves very differently from the familiar clockwork universe. Subatomic particles called leptons can exist in two places at the same time. In the vast expanse of the universe, the shortest distance between two points is not necessarily a straight line. Scientists are proving many of these bizarre ideas, yet in the day-to-day world, people assume there is nothing new to discover.

I believe that the world outside and the world within are intrinsically linked. I would go so far as to say that they are one and the same, and that thinking influences—perhaps even determines—what happens. As you think, so you become.

Jung wrote his theory of synchronicity to tackle this problem of the relationship between the inner and outer worlds. He showed a correlation between inner and outer events. In his autobiography, *Memories, Dreams, Reflections*, he quotes a number of instances where mysterious coincidences corresponded with important spiritual turning points of his own, and with patients' inner development. He showed that the world of dreams can sometimes find expression in unexpected coincidences.

What if the events that happen in the world are influenced by your thoughts, dreams, and fantasies? The responsibility for your suffering and your problems would then lie squarely on your own shoulders. Your troubles—even those thrust upon you unexpectedly—are of your own making. Not only are you the victim of your own thoughts, but you have the potential to make the world into whatever you wish it to be if you learn how to use your thoughts and fantasies the right way. Fantasy may not therefore be wishful thinking, but a powerful psychological tool that can be used to improve the world.

## The Secret Power of Fantasy

Thoughts are very important because all consciousness is connected together and thoughts can influence other people and the world in general. Thoughts are things.

Thoughts also interact with what some have called the Universal Mind. This is the consciousness that lies behind all things—you could call it God, I suppose. When a thought goes out, it enters the Universal Mind, which in turn influences the events that happen in life. It follows that if you wish for something enough it will eventually come into your life.

Many people go through life without giving a thought to why they are here. Their focus is perhaps on having a family or getting a good job. Many people live life without ever being aware that there are other possibilities. They live a life that is satisfactory but have very little knowledge of their true potential. They may never feel the thrill of inspiration when they see something beautiful; they may never look at the stars and wonder at the magnificence of the universe; they may never think about the meaning of human life and whether there is an afterlife. For this sort of person, life is something that just happens, over which they have very little control. In many ways they are like animals. They are sentient beings, but their consciousness is only partially awake.

Most of us have a degree of this in our own lives. We fall into routine and blame the world when things go wrong. But we all have a higher nature waiting to awaken. For some it may take many more rebirths; for others, the calling to full consciousness happens in this lifetime. It may come from a series of events in the real world, such as a tragic event that makes the person reconsider the purpose of life, or it may come from within spontaneously. When it happens, the process of becoming activates within the person and the person embarks on the inner exploration of the unconscious.

But this inner search for wholeness also influences the exterior world. The inner challenges may have similar counterparts in the real world. Others who have embarked on the spiritual path talk about feeling challenged as soon as they began their spiritual work. I certainly found this when I became a medium. I was faced with the difficult prospect of becoming a professional medium or continuing to make a fortune from my advertising and design business. I chose mediumship. Other people following their spiritual path have lost their jobs, seen their relationships break up, seen people they love die, or suffered serious illnesses themselves. The path toward consciousness is truly the journey of the hero.

In most cases we are not aware of what has happened until after the event. When we reflect upon the adversity that may have come into our lives in the past we see that there was a call for change within ourselves. If we dealt with it correctly we may understand that adversity has molded us into the people we are now. Transformation does not

happen in a comfy armchair, it comes from suffering. The sword is made in the fire, between the hammer and the anvil. Adverse events happen because most people do not consciously decide to improve themselves. So the transformation is brought to them by destiny.

The benefit of becoming conscious is that you start to take responsibility for your life. At first you may modify your behavior and the things you say to others. As you become self-aware, you understand what things hurt you, and you try not to harm others the same way. You begin to watch your thoughts and feelings and may use techniques such as meditation to discipline yourself. Eventually you become the master of your personality and character. By taking control of your life, you may avoid many of the trials that come into the lives of people who are not on the spiritual path.

When you learn to control your fate in this way, you see that the hardships that have come into your life have been created by yourself over many past lifetimes. Karma has followed you into this life and needs to be worked out. Karma is the law of cause and effect. It is the natural law that was described by Jesus when he said, "As ye sow, so shall ye reap." Similarly, in the Old Testament it says, "...they that plough iniquity and sow wickedness, reap the same" (Job 4:8). And at least 50 years before the birth of Christ, the Roman statesman, philosopher, and orator Cicero, said, "As you have sown, so shall you reap." A more modern way to express this ancient

CREATE AN ATTITUDE OF WINNING

wisdom is found in the phrase "What goes around, comes around."

In the Koran, it says, "Have you considered what you sow?" [The Event 56.63]. The given wisdom is that karma is created by our actions: you hurt someone now, and sometime in the future—maybe in a future life—you will be hurt in a similar way. You may sow anger, kindness, hate, love, envy, prejudice—whatever quality you bring to bear will be returned to you. Good and bad actions will bring good and bad results. Just as a farmer sows seeds and gains a crop, so you will reap more than you sow. It is an immutable law of nature with as much force as the law of gravity.

But the most powerful karmic influence is not your actions. It is your thoughts. Right now they are creating your future. The way you think attracts good or bad fortune. "When it rains it pours," say some people, and "bad luck comes in threes." What terrible luck are these people drawing into their lives? What are you doing to yourself when you say, "This job is killing me"? Could you be bringing illness into your life with these unconscious affirmations in your daily language?

This is where fantasy can help. By consciously creating the right images in your head, you start to influence your happiness now and your circumstances in the future. Fantasy can become a tool that will help you become the master of your life. You can use fantasy to establish new patterns of behavior that will not only be of benefit to yourself but will help others. You will become happy, and it will rub off on everyone you meet. And most importantly, you will be creating an invisible influence of thought that will change everything around you.

## Using Positive Fantasy

What is the first thing you do if you want a new pair of shoes? Answer: You picture the shoes in your mind. Everything starts with a thought. The thought triggers the action and you can earn the money and go to the store and buy what you need. All things in life start with a thought. A great painting is visualized in the mind of an artist. A scientist first thinks about his invention before anything physical is constructed.

For many people, the fear of disappointment can become a stumbling block that stops them from fulfilling their fantasy vision of how they would like things to be. Instead of a positive vision of the future, fear may cause them to dismiss it as unattainable. A relationship fails and you may expect all future relationships to fail. After a financial crisis, you may expect always to be poor. Failure habits can all too easily become ingrained into your subconscious.

The answer is to reprogram the subconscious and create new habits of thinking and expectation. The subconscious does not listen to reason. It listens to repetition. So write yourself a simple positive command that expresses what you want, and repeat it to yourself as much as possible and particularly as you go to sleep. For example, if you are ill you may use a positive affirmation such as: "I am one with the eternal. I draw from the infinite source for health, strength, and vitality. I am whole. Perfect health is mine to have." Similarly, if you have obstacles in your way you can repeat: "I have the power to overcome any difficulty I may encounter, and I give myself permission for my life to become whatever I want it to be." If your problems are getting you down, you could say: "It is my divine right to be happy. I am happy now and will be for all eternity."

Spiritual healing is particularly influenced by the images and fantasies you have while healing is taking place. If you think positive thoughts while you are ill, it will trigger chemicals in the brain to aid your recovery. Happy imagery will encourage you to get well. Many hospitals now recognize the importance of positive imagery and hang paintings filled with optimistic imagery and bright colors in the wards. Similarly, some healers encourage patients to watch comedies to help to maintain an optimistic and positive attitude of mind that in turn influences the healing process. As they say: "Laughter is the best medicine."

Having positive thoughts is crucial when giving healing to others. I explain to my healing students how to stimulate and move the spiritual energies that bring healing. However, I stress that the thoughts they are having will also influence the healing process. If they have happy fantasies about the person being well and in perfect health, it will improve the quality of the healing energy that will be influenced and charged by these thoughts. When I work with my healing students, we sometimes use a guided fantasy meditation at the outset of healing, sending healing thoughts to our patients in the form of a fantasy. For example, for absent healing, we visualize the people who need healing sitting around a crystal fountain in a beautiful garden. In our imagination we bathe them in light and happiness. Never do we see the illness, only the health. Using this technique we are able to send healing over any distance—and it works.

The healing energy is guided by thought. In some healing systems, such as Reiki, the healing is directed using set symbols. This will also work. My own personal preference is to work with the imagery that is given spontaneously from the unconscious. Often these impromptu fantasies contain the right imagery and colors for the particular illness being treated. Whatever method you use, the important thing is to maintain a positive state of mind while healing. For many people, a happy fantasy is the best method to achieve this.

Affirmations and positive fantasies such as these will change the way you think. Instead of looking at problems as things difficult to solve, you may now see them as added opportunities for developing fortitude and spiritual healing power. To build your own personal power, here are a few simple points you would be wise to adopt:

***Build Confidence.*** A simple way to influence your own subconscious habits is to project an attitude of total self-confidence, no matter what happens. You may be screaming with worry inside, but act as if there is nothing bothering you and you can deal with anything life throws at you. This technique will trick your subconscious into actually being the positive, unruffled person you would like to be, and the subtle signals you unconsciously display with your body language and facial expressions will influence the people around you.

USING THE SENSE OF SMELL

There are also many ways to enhance this self-confident state of mind. Buying new clothes before a job interview or a date can reinforce your positive feelings. Put photographs around your house that remind you of times when you were happy or made an achievement. These images will subconsciously remind you of your successes. Certain music may have positive associations. And don't forget the sense of smell. The fragrance of roses may remind you of the first time you fell in love. An old-fashioned perfume sprayed onto a handkerchief may remind you of happy times from childhood. You may have many personal associations with certain smells. They can be used to reinforce your happiest memories. By letting go of your failures and reinforcing your happy memories and your memories of success, you will automatically become more self-confident.

**Look Ahead.** Most people worry too much about the past and future. A large portion of their psychological energy is wasted. To cope with these worries it is sensible to remove them from your thinking and to look ahead with a feeling of positive expectation. Salesmen are well aware of the importance of setting goals to reach their target. You can apply the same techniques to your life. Write yourself a list of what you want to achieve from life. First write your "today" list. Make it realistic and achievable, and do the most difficult task first. It is tremendously encouraging seeing each task crossed off. At a glance you can see how much you really do achieve.

Make a long-term list also. Set an achievable goal for the week, for the months ahead, and for the years in the future. Big goals, such as owning a new home, may be listed a long way ahead. But set a time limit. Stick to it and work hard toward your goal. Plan ahead and know that what you really want **will** come to you.

**The Language of Fantasy.** The unconscious mind will respond to verbal commands used in affirmations. For many people, this is the easiest way to begin influencing the way they think and feel. An even more powerful technique is to speak to the unconscious in its own language. This language is the same language expressed in dreams—metaphor, allegory, and symbolism. We can speak to the unconscious by using fantasy, particularly if the fantasy also contains symbolism. You must "experience" the achievement of your goal using fantasy. If you can do this, you will not only influence your behavior in a positive way but will also encourage the right "coincidences" to happen to you. Once you know the goal, the inner and outer worlds will synchronize in order for us to attain that goal.

## USING FANTASY TO INFLUENCE THE FUTURE

*"The best way to predict the future is to invent it."*

ALAN KAY

I was touched by the story the Dalai Lama told about leaving Tibet when the Chinese invaded. As he and his entourage hastily left the Potala Palace in Lhasa to begin their escape to India, the Dalai Lama insisted they pause for a moment. He then visualized an image of the entourage safely arriving in India. Then he visualized them safely returning one day to Tibet. By doing this, the Dalai Lama created the right energy for it to happen eventually. At the time of this writing the Dalai Lama remains in exile, but one day the Tibetan people will be free and the Dalai Lama will be able to return to his homeland. The image has already been given to the Universal Mind.

The point of this example is that you must carry a vision within. It is important to do this when you set out on a long journey but also important for your journey in life. The next experiment will use fantasy—or should I say visions—to help you achieve what you need in life. You can do this exercise whenever you wish.

### Experiment

**Step 1:** First you must think about what it is that you want to achieve in life. This is the most important stage of all. What is it that you REALLY want? As they say, "Be careful what you wish for, for it will surely happen."

**Step 2:** Make the wish specific. It's no good just wishing to be rich or happy. You need to think of a specific goal. For example I may wish that this book will become a bestseller. I have a clear target that I can focus on and use. Think of something specific that you wish to achieve. It may be an emotional goal, such as meeting the perfect partner, or something spiritual, such as developing healing powers. Choose whatever you want for your goal but in this instance keep to just one. You can set other goals in future tries.

**Step 3:** Now that you have a specific goal, turn it into a picture form so that it will influence the unconscious mind. Close your eyes and picture yourself achieving the goal. Can you picture it? If you cannot see it, you may have obstacles within yourself that are preventing you from having the vision. Give yourself permission for the vision to come to you. Can you picture yourself achieving the goal? See yourself achieving it.

**Step 4:** If you can picture yourself achieving the goal, you will know it is a goal that is possible to achieve. You have the vision. Before you can achieve anything in life, you must first have the vision. So whatever you wish to achieve, first get the vision. Before writing this book I had a vision of what it would be. Every time I sat down to write I closed my eyes and visualized the work for that day completed. You are now reading the vision I had.

**Step 5:** Know that you can do the same in your own life. You can bring about whatever you want. Now get completely immersed in the vision. Experience the whole scenario. As you achieve your goal, what feelings do you have? What do you see around you? Have people in your fantasy complimenting you for reaching your goal, or admiring your new "thing," being happy for you, etc. What do the faces of the people who may be with you say about your success? What can you hear? What sensory feelings do you have? Let the success vision become all-embracing.

**Step 6:** Next, give the vision to the Universal Mind (or God, if you prefer). You give it to the universe asking in your heart that the vision may come to reality. See the vision moving away from you. Now, move the picture to the left or right—depending on "where" your brain considers the "future" to be. (To find out what direction this is for you, think of something that happened yesterday. Notice in which direction your eyes move, even if it's only slightly. If it is to the right, your past is the right, and your future is to the left. If it's to the left, your past is to the left, and your future is to the right.) The vision has become part of the future of the Universal Mind and WILL come into your life.

**Step 7:** Now clear your mind and ask the unconscious to give you a symbol to carry with you. For example, if you asked that you might have courage, you may see the image of a sword. As a writer I may see a magic pen that writes only wonderful words. You may see all sorts of peculiar imagery. Choose from what you are given and think of it from time to time as a promise from the Universal Mind. You may want to think about the image when you feel you need reassuring and may even draw it, write about it, or sing songs about it. Use the symbol as a fantasy daydream.

**Step 8:** Now forget it, and set about finding ways to make that vision happen. It probably won't drop in your lap but now your efforts are more likely to bear fruit. If you truly believe in the vision you have, it will certainly come about. Sometimes it takes a slightly different form from what you expected, but the essence of what you have wished for will come into your life.

**Step 9:** Reinforce your vision by thinking of the symbols you were given during the day. Before going to sleep each night, picture in the psychic center in the middle of the forehead an image of what you want. Move toward it and experience living out your heart's wish. Imagine that it has already happened. Build the image. Sense the colors, smells, and sounds, and know deep in your heart that the goal you are visualizing is coming to you.

## HOW SOON WILL MY LIFE CHANGE?

*"I find that the harder I work, the more luck I seem to have."*

THOMAS JEFFERSON (1743-1826)

Psychics and mystics believe that we are all part of a universal mind. This spiritual Internet can be influenced by your thoughts, which connect you to this powerful network. If you broadcast your desires without selfishness, you attract good fortune into your life. In particular, during meditation or prayer super-conscious powers come into play. I would argue that everything you wish for eventually comes about—in this life or in future lives.

So why is life so bad? The troubles you have now are caused by your past thinking! The bad mental vibrations and fantasies you had in the past are influencing your life now. You are creating new energy every day that will eventually create your future conditions. If you have been forever fantasizing about pessimistic scenarios, they are likely to become part of your life one day. Similarly, the good fantasies and positive thoughts you have are creating good fortune. In the final analysis, you cannot blame anyone else, destiny, or God for your predicament because you have created your own circumstances.

The good and bad actions you have done in your past create the same mental energy. For example, the negative thoughts you may have if you deliberately harm someone will rebound on you, as will the thoughts of the person who has been harmed. All that happens in the world is simply the unfolding of karma.

So if you want to help yourself and others you should start right away by adjusting your thinking. Sometimes the effects of your positive fantasy will be immediate and you will see positive changes in your life. However, in most instances there has to be a clearing of the past negative thinking first before the new, benevolent cycle can begin. Nonetheless, you can still use the "bad" situations to your advantage. If you can accept that you are the cause of all that befalls you, you will no longer feel that destiny or bad luck is punishing you. With the right attitude, difficult circumstances can become your best teacher.

Imagine what it would be like if everything you wished for came about immediately. There would be chaos. It is essential that good and bad karma

be given time to unfold. Similarly, the positive fantasies you have now may not bring their benefit until the time is right. However if you can make positive fantasy part of your way of life rather than a momentary thought, the effects will be with you much sooner. Positive fantasy needs to become an ingrained habit. Whenever you begin a task, have a vision of it in your mind completed in the best possible way. Imagine yourself feeling pleased with your accomplishments.

Positive fantasy techniques can be applied to even the smallest tasks. Eventually you will establish a completely new state of mind that is focused on finding solutions. This also affects the way you react to people and you will create an ambience of success in your aura. This will in turn affect how people react to you, and can even influence your health. A generally positive frame of mind will certainly have an effect on you and will help you deal with your problems and in general gain a better perspective.

These fantasy techniques can certainly be used to improve your own attitude to your situation. However, in a magical way fantasies may also influence other people and the flow of events that happen in your life. Given that external events sometimes synchronize with inner conditions, it follows that it is possible to influence events by your thoughts and fantasies. A fantasy that is generating good positive energy will draw good fortune into your life.

# Index

## About the Author

Craig Hamilton-Parker is a celebrated medium who has confounded skeptics with the uncanny accuracy of his readings. The author of numerous books, including the bestsellers *The Hidden Meaning of Dreams*, *The Psychic Casebook*, *Remembering Your Dreams*, and *What To Do When You Are Dead*, he writes columns and articles for newspapers and magazines around the world. His website, www.psychics.co.uk, attracts a community of experts who meet in its chatrooms for regular debates and practice.